STUDIES IN AFRICAN LITERATURE

The Novels of Ayi Kwei Armah

Studies in African Literature

The Novels of
Ayi Kwei Armah

A STUDY IN POLEMICAL FICTION

Robert Fraser

LONDON
HEINEMANN
IBADAN NAIROBI

Heinemann Educational Books Ltd
22 Bedford Square, London WC1B 3HH
P.M.B. 5205, Ibadan · P.O. Box 45314, Nairobi

EDINBURGH   MELBOURNE   AUCKLAND
HONG KONG   SINGAPORE   KUALA LUMPUR   NEW DELHI
KINGSTON   PORT OF SPAIN

Heinemann Educational Books Inc.
4 Front Street, Exeter, New Hampshire 03833, USA

ISBN 0 435 91300 X (cased)
ISBN 0 435 91301 8 (paper)

Set, printed and bound in Great Britain by
Fakenham Press Limited, Fakenham, Norfolk

For John Mapondera, Irene and the Drum Arts Centre

Contents

▼▼▼▼▼▼▼▼▼▼▼▼▼▼▼▼▼▼▼▼▼▼▼▼▼▼▼▼▼▼

Preface

The title of this book may need some explanation. Ayi Kwei Armah has written short stories, poetry and some astringent political criticism. It is as a novelist, however, that he is best known, and it is with this aspect of his work that I have contented myself, since it is here that his talent is both most evident and most experimental.

This limitation of scope has certain advantages. An exceptionally innovative artist, it is in his novels that Armah has made the most emphatic and bracing departures. Commencing within the realm of realistic social fiction, he has gradually released himself from its restraints to lead the novel, his chosen medium, into new and unfamiliar pastures. This study, then, embraces two related aims. It is both an estimate of a writer, and an essay in the evolution of a literary form.

The African novel has an interesting history. Though possessing well attested roots in the vernacular oral traditions, the tendency of those of its exponents who write either in English or in French has been to neglect these in favour of formal structures which derive from elsewhere. There are notable exceptions to this: the use of folktale in Achebe's novels, for instance, or the remarkable prose sagas of Amos Tutuola. Nevertheless the generalization holds that the challenging content of much contemporary African narrative has not always been matched by an equivalent daring in its formal structure. This is less a matter of technique narrowly conceived than of authorial voice, the way in which the writer perceives himself in relation to the reader, and his consequent manner of address.

It is therefore a welcome and arresting change to approach the work of a contemporary novelist from West Africa who, though beginning in a time-honoured mould, has latterly taken a shrewd look at the place of the writer in the current African setting, and from it seemingly drawn certain conclusions as to the function and duty of the prose artist, conclusions which may cause discomfort, but which nevertheless merit close scrutiny and debate. From his first emergence in 1968 as the author of the justly acclaimed *The Beautyful Ones Are Not Yet Born*, Ayi Kwei Armah has been seen as a startling writer, a fearless and unpredictable enfant terrible at drastic odds with the literary establishment. The sense of shock with which his first book was greeted was, however, decidedly more of a reaction to its content and imagery than to its form. Recently, however, his art has evolved in new and flamboyant directions which none but his most astute earlier readers could possibly have predicted. In the context of an energetic and challenging writer's career this is perhaps not altogether surprising: technical development after all is one of the salient signs of progress. Yet, if the performance of twentieth-century writers is anything to go by, the usual direction of change is towards greater complexity and a more opaque texture. Armah presents us with a marked exception to this rule. His work has in no sense become harder. He is not one of those artists – James Joyce might serve as an example – whose work becomes more hermetic or convoluted as it develops. Rather the opposite: Armah's prose style has become increasingly transparent, the amount of ambiguity, for example, having notably declined. This cannot be taken, as it might be with writers working in other circumstances, as a sign of any lessening of control. Rather is it a result of something much more interesting. Since his removal to Julius Nyerere's Tanzania, and more recently to Lesotho, Armah has evidently become increasingly concerned with the democratic basis of his art. There has been a marked effort to reach out beyond the confines of the literati and the university intelligentsia to the larger potential reading public, and hence hopefully to recapture some of the wider ancestral appeal of the oral artist. The translation of *The Beautyful Ones Are Not Yet Born* into Swahili, the lingua franca of East Africa, might be taken as one instance of this. The relative directness and wide appeal of his later novels must be seen as another. The directions which his style and narrative manner have taken can hence be viewed, not so much as the result of pressures which have accumulated within the art itself, as the product of a growing awareness of the social context within which the professional artist in Africa must operate.

Just as his consciousness of the needs of a wider audience have caused Armah to revise the stylistic emphasis of his art, so has it resulted, more radically perhaps, in his altering its informing sensibility. Critics of his early work had a tendency to upbraid him for a morbid and sterile preoccupation with the harrowing position of the artist figure isolated in an unsympathetic environment. To some extent this is true, and in this respect his first few books showed a certain dependence on notions and obsessions arising ultimately from the European Romantic tradition. Recently, however, Armah's orientation in this respect has notably changed. The artist figure disappears, or is merged in a wider professional group or guild. Simultaneously the emphasis on the recreation of individual states of mind recedes, to the extent that Armah can now be regarded pre-eminently as the craftsman of the plural voice, the communal consciousness, the racial memory. Acute readers may have detected a tendency in this direction in the earlier books – what, after all, is the long reminiscence sequence in Chapter 6 of *The Beautyful Ones* but an exploration of the communal memory? Nevertheless it can be stated without exaggeration that the development of the collective voice observable in the later books amounts to a revolution, not only in Armah's art in particular, but for the African novel in general.

As Armah had readjusted his priorities, so it is incumbent on the sympathetic critic who is concerned with his work to adjust his. Armah himself has very firm ideas on the function of the critic:

> The key to the skillful interpreter's role lies in his relationship with his audience. The skillful interpreter functions in close tune with the allergies, aspirations, ideals, manias, philias, phobias and prejudices – above all the prejudices – of his audience. The skillful interpreter knows how to respect and protect his audience's prejudices. Operating almost by instinct, he censors information before he transmits it.
>
> If any of this information threatens to clash too pointedly with his audience's sensibilities, he prudently blunts its point and turns it harmlessly aside, if he cannot bury it altogether. And if any particular item of information flatters his audience's sensibilities, he strengthens its impact. If any item reinforces his audience's prejudices, he sharpens its point. If there is a shortage of flattering information, the really skillful interpreter creates useable items of surrogate information. The skillful interpreter, in short, does not allow information to ruffle his audience's sensibilities. He uses information to reinforce his audience's prejudices.*

The critic then is a kind of sieve, a protective device intended to shield his society from indigestible truths. If the creative writer aims at a kind of self-knowledge, then the critic masks this with a more palatable self-deception. While this verdict may be over-harsh in its simplification, it is particularly pertinent to the sort of critical treatment which Armah's own work has received. For he is never a comfortable author to read, and an attentive response to his work is likely to raise qualms in the most hardened breast. Africa he constantly accuses of self-betrayal; Europe of downright oppression. Nobody likes to be on the receiving end of such salutary, bitter truths, and thus it is that the cultural reflexes of the critical fraternity have by and large worked to exclude what they could not accommodate, and to transform what seems unacceptable in its rigour. This is equally true wherever his work has been read or assessed. Those who have had the opportunity of discussing his work both in the West and in Africa will have discovered simultaneous symptoms of acceptance and rejection in both contexts. None of us wishes to face up to the direst consequences of our mutual colonial past, of which we are all –

* From 'Larsony or fiction as criticism of fiction', *Asemka* (Cape Coast) no. 4, reprinted in Ife, Nigeria, *The Positive Review*, no. 1 (1978), p. 11.

colonized and colonizer alike – the blinkered victims. Armah's work, if attended to, can tell us much, not merely about the world in which we live, but about the reasons which might cause us at first to be suspicious of much that is to be found in his novels. It is crucial to the argument of this study that the critical resistance to Armah's books to date has been part and parcel of the cultural dislocation which they portray.

There is another, related difficulty. As already explained, the whole emphasis of Armah's work has recently shifted to a communal axis. Now the technique of literary criticism as presently practised in the Western world, and by adoption in most of the universities and other circles of discussion in Africa, is undeniably the product of the individualistic, humanist strain which has been dominant in European culture since the Renaissance. More specifically, in the English-speaking world, the formative influences have been, whether we like it or not, those that have arisen from the Puritan Protestant stream in the life of the country where the language itself originated. It should be immediately obvious that the driving impulses behind Armah's writing run totally counter to this stream at practically every point. He has, as far as I can see, very few links either with England or with its literature, his non-African allegiances in so far as he has cultivated them, being American or, more decidedly, French. Despite the tone of individual anguish in his first three books, his primary concern has been with the cultivation of the collective, rather than the individual sensibility. His essential theme has been the process through which a nation may force its way back to a state of natural health after a prolonged period of spiritual infection. He is thus concerned with the salvation of the people in toto, the reformation of the public will, rather than the redemption of the private soul or mind. In certain places in his work this change of emphasis surfaces and achieves systematic definition. A remarkable case of this is the religious debate in the second novel, *Fragments*, in which Baako and Juana, two of the principal characters, discuss the relative claims of the Protestant and Catholic modes of salvation. Baako comes down decisively on the side of the Catholic doctrine, and, in so doing, provides a perspective on the whole novel in which the entire notion of man's spiritual destiny is seen in terms of the salvation of the community attempting to wrestle some meaning out of the rubble of their fallen state. It would, of course, be a profound error to call Armah a Catholic writer, but in this narrow and quite specific sense the category is quite meaningful. More than this, however, he is an African writer who has faced up to the most challenging consequences of his professional position, and modelled his writing increasingly with these in mind. The effort must therefore be to account for his work in these terms.

I do hope that I have not been guilty of making more extravagant claims for this brief study than I am capable of sustaining. I would have got nowhere without the energy and stimulus of several of my ex-students and colleagues who have discussed Armah's work with me along the way. Particular thanks are due to Martin Owusu and Mary Nicholson at Cape Coast, and, at Leeds, Martin Banham and Dr Loreto Todd, who supplied me with invaluable technical advice on Armah's language. Also a third-year student who on one bleak and wintry Yorkshire morning alerted me to the cinematic affinities of Armah's art. Lastly, I wish to honour the memory of another former colleague, John Chantler, who, had he not been killed in a road accident some years ago, might have given us a very astute book on Armah.

1 The Context: Liberation and Resistance

▼▼▼▼▼▼▼▼▼▼▼▼▼▼▼▼▼▼▼▼▼▼▼▼▼▼▼▼▼▼▼▼

AYI Kwei Armah is one of the most controversial writers Africa has produced. From 1968, the date of the publication of his first book, *The Beautyful Ones Are Not Yet Born*, to the present when, after ten years of endeavour, he has completed five novels, his reputation has been clouded by misunderstanding and a kind of critical irrelevance that have denied him the recognition his originality would seem to demand. Not one single commentator has denied the sheer force of his talent. Even those who accuse him of impudence are forced to register the distinction of his style, his 'eloquent prose', the dexterity of his organization.[1] Yet there remains a reluctance to grant the seminal nature of his contribution that would seem to spring from nervous embarrassment at the vital issues his writing has so consistently and inconveniently raised.

To some extent this situation is a result of his somewhat eccentric publishing history. Editions of his first novel appeared on both sides of the Atlantic within a few months of one another, and were extensively reviewed on three continents. His next novel, *Fragments*, appeared in America two years after the first, but was not issued by a British publisher until 1974. Since, due to international copyright agreements, copies were also difficult to obtain in Africa, this impressive work has not been taken widely into account until comparatively recently. His fourth book *Two Thousand Seasons* is published by the East African Publishing House, but possessed for some time no British edition. The unfortunate result of all this has been to confine the attention of readers and critics largely to Armah's celebrated debut, *The Beautyful Ones Are Not Yet Born*,[2] without any systematic attempt being made to place the asperity of that work within a broader picture of the writer's vision.

We are now, perhaps for the first time, in a position to be able to correct this imbalance, and to ask ourselves the question, what kind of a writer has Armah demonstrated himself to be? His early reviewers had a marked tendency to consign his work a little too glibly to a genre which Arthur Ravenscroft had earlier termed 'novels of disillusion'.[3] Political earnestness, a disenchantment with the leadership with which African countries have had to contend since independence, a visceral writhing at public hypocrisy: all of these were seized on as conclusive characteristics. Cynicism was taken to be the controlling point of view. Indeed, much of the existing criticism has tended to make of Armah a sort of decadently prurient nihilist 'trapped' as one reviewer put it 'in the vainglorious contemplation of the righteous self'.[4]

A more comprehensive reading of his works to date serves totally to disarm this earlier impression. That Armah is a profoundly moral writer few would feel able to deny. But to construe his morality to be of the narrow, carping variety is totally to misread his novels, to take the delicate sensibility informing them for something infinitely nastier and less wholesome. A comparison sometimes cited is that to a doctor,[5] but the detached surgeon wielding a sterilized scalpel would seem to be less appropriate than a discerning practitioner whose concern embraces the entire personality of the patient. There is a marked therapeutic value to much of Armah's work. We can now see that he is concerned fundamentally with the ethical quality of a nation's life, a potential for exuberant health he sees as having been strangled by an infection of foreign origin.[6] In the first two books we were treated to some rather gruesome medical illustrations. Increasingly, however, his vigilance has directed itself less to the pallor invading the surface than to the causes lurking beyond immediate notice, the sad aetiology of their growth.

Latterly this has involved Armah in a consideration of causes that lie in the recent or remoter past. Yet, if one returns to the earlier novels, one can see this tendency already latent. Trained in the social sciences, he has always been fascinated by the forces making for social change. In a sense his imagination is of an historical order, not in the ways applicable to the historian or even the historical novelist proper, but rather as one whose mind dwells on tracts of human experience in search of a clue to the depredation visited on his people. Fundamentally, this search has been a pragmatic affair. Though tempted by alien ideologies, he has largely steered clear of them in an attempt to forge an individual view of his society's development. Despite a lengthy period of residence in the West, he is deeply suspicious of conceptual systems deriving from Europe, all the more so, perhaps, because some of his work retains vestiges of their influence. To the extent that he has been influenced by others, he shows some sign, rare in an anglophone author, of indebtedness to francophone writing. Certainly his absorption with theoretical problems reminds one more of the French school of thought than the English, a characteristic which links him less with the Nigerians, Achebe and Soyinka, than with the Senegalese novelist and film director, Sembene Ousmane.

It is impossible, however, to understand his pressing concerns without considering the generation in which he came to maturity, together with the turmoil into which his own society, in common with many others in the so-called Third World has been plunged in the last forty years. Armah's imagination is of the sort which habitually makes connections between different times and places. Seeing himself as an oppressed man, he is able to reach out to those he believes share his plight. His consciousness of the nature of repression and change has therefore been dictated by the resurgence of the colonized peoples in the 1950s and 1960s, and to a certain extent by the theoretical critiques to which this has given rise. It will be instructive, therefore, to take a brief look at the course of his career to date, with an eye to the experiences and influences to which he has in turn been subjected.

Nationalist Politics, 1939–59

Ayi Kwei Armah was born to Fante-speaking parents at Sekondi Takoradi, the twin harbour city in the West of Ghana, in 1939. The year of his birth places him within a generation whose experience of the political development of West Africa is unique. In 1939 the then Gold Coast was on the brink of a war in which her interests seemed only marginally to be involved, but as a result of which thousands of her young men were sent to death and mutilation in Burma or elsewhere. At the armistice the troop-ships in the harbour disgorged whole platoons of men whose experience of the outside world had enlarged their political vision, but whose ambitions were immediately thwarted by the chronic unemployment of the late 1940s. Economic disappointment soon turned to social unrest. Already, organized labour had started flexing its arm. The year 1942 alone saw ten strikes.[7] As a result British trades union officials were sent out from London in the following year with a brief to set up legal associations. Takoradi, with the large workforce employed by the communications network, was very prominent in these developments. In 1950, in response to Nkrumah's call for 'Positive Action', the whole port ground to a halt for a twelve-day period. It was not long before aspirations took a more decisively political turn. In 1947, a small group of eminent lawyers had set up the United Gold Coast Convention (UGCC), which soon started holding rallies in Takoradi township. These, however, were moderate men, with a stake in the status quo, and their demands were soon outpaced by Kwame Nkrumah, who initially joined their number as Secretary-General, but soon broke away to form his own Congress People's Party (CPP). Nkrumah's personal style, informal, demotic, intensely energetic, was very appealing to young people of

Armah's generation, who soon swelled the nationalist movement in droves.

One might have thought Armah too young to have taken in much of the import of that period, if it were not for the long reminiscence sequence that makes up the sixth chapter of his first novel *The Beautyful Ones Are Not Yet Born*. The point seems to be that Armah was not only historically, but also geographically, well placed to observe what was happening. A sea port is a fine vantage point from which to view the stirrings of a nation under stress. In that book Teacher and 'the man' share a common boyhood and adolescence, a common experience of the dejection of their elders during the savage anticlimax of peace, common aspirations fed first by the besuited 'jokers' with their derisory attempts at agitation, then by Nkrumah's wonderful emergence, someone who at last voiced their cause with dignity, a man speaking to men. They also share the subsequent desolation of those hopes due to the history of independent Ghana, leading to the kind of disappointment which has instilled Armah's own writing with an eloquent despair very characteristic of him as an artist.

His early education was undertaken in Ghana at Achimota College, the school set up near Accra by Governor Guggesberg in 1922 as a deliberate élite-creating institution along the lines of the British public schools. It is worthwhile emphasizing this because, in order to appreciate the tone of much of Armah's writing, it is important to realize that, by training though not by temperament, he is part of that Ghanaian élite whose predicament his works so pertinently analyse. His protest is not tinged by the resentment of the social outcast; it is rather the gesture of someone who has meticulously rejected the fruits of conformity palpably within his grasp. Despite its patrician atmosphere, the school was beginning to feel the ripples of unrest. The youth of the country had always been in the vanguard of nationalist commitment. Indeed it was a meeting of youth organizations which had initially forced Nkrumah's hand in setting up his own party.[8] At Achimota, Nkrumah's own alma mater, feelings ran high. To quote David Apter, 'Secondary school students at Achimota, who were in the nucleus of trained and aggressive but responsible political leadership in the Gold Coast, provided a solidarity grouping which cut across traditional kinship and authority ties.'[9]

Armah, however, was not to stay in this atmosphere for very long. In 1959 he won a scholarship which took him to America, first to Groton School and then to Harvard. He was now to withdraw from the Ghanaian scene for seven years, crucial years these for the political integrity of black Africa, a testing ground for her newest republic. He must have carried away a profound impression of the future seemingly promised to his country. Ghana had been independent for two years. Despite the ominous Preventive Detention Act of 1958, it was still another two years before establishment of a one-party state. Osagyefo Nkrumah was beginning to display himself in the international arena in which he assumed the mantle of his continent's champion. It is well to bear in mind the hopes an ardent student must have carried away from this scene when we attempt to understand the feelings of disillusionment evoked in his first three novels.

America and Black Revolution

Both at this time and later, Armah spent several years in American academia: as high-school student, undergraduate at Harvard, from which he graduated 'Summa cum laude' in sociology, later at Columbia and, briefly, on the staff of the University of Massachusetts. More important, however, is the political education he evidently underwent in the States. His years there correspond almost exactly to the most turbulent period in recent black American politics. It was then that the Kennedy and Johnson administrations felt the full brunt of the Civil Rights Movement which did so much to induce self-respect and political solidarity among people of African descent. The experience of confrontation of a more stridently racial variety combined with the candid rhetoric of revolt can be seen to have affected Armah's thinking positively. To summarize, this is observable in two ways. First there is his deep ingrained suspicion of the self-defensive antics by means of which a white élite attempts to bolster up its supremacy. One can see this, for example, in *Why Are We So Blest?* in one scene in which the Ghanaian Modin, the most closely autobiographical of the characters, encounters a complacent white fellow-student who reads out to him a Thanksgiving Day article from one of the Sunday newspapers. The sheer indulgence of Armah's parody of its swelling prose would seem to suggest his attitude towards the more banal instances of white apologetics.[10] Secondly, there is the strongly embedded belief that black people must carve out their own destiny independent of the corrosive influences of white contact. Historically, this insight derives from the writings of the Jamaican thinker Marcus Garvey (1887–1940), a man whose philosophy also influenced Nkrumah. There was, however, a marked revival of such thinking in the 1960s, finding its ultimate expression in the Black Muslim Movement. Again, and particularly in the fourth novel, *Two Thousand Seasons*, Armah constantly returns to the notion of complete separation as the only possible means of black salvation.

Recognizing the extent of Armah's revolutionary allegiances, one is called upon to explain the tone of despondency with the aftermath of political action in most of his novels. There is no doubt of his absolute commitment to the cause of the subjected races; yet the Ghana of *The Beautyful Ones* and the Algeria of *Why Are We So Blest?* are both places whose recent emancipation has led straight to sterility. One is here clearly faced with the question of time-scale. For Armah, as for many at this period, the African revolution was a matter of strict necessity. So much was axiomatic and time has done little to mitigate its force. However, in the heady atmosphere of that time, it must have seemed not only necessary, but also imminent. Schooled as Armah was on Nkrumah's peremptory and effective demands for 'Self Government Now' together with the teachings of men like Malcolm X that the bastion of white supremacy was fatally breached and about to fall, it must have appeared that the hour of reckoning was nigh. To adapt the title of his first novel, the 'beautyful ones' seemed not only to be born but actually storming the battlements. However, as the 1960s dragged themselves into the 1970s, and the American radicals settled for compromise, and Ghana for mediocrity, the dawn of liberty seemed to have retreated. Much of Armah's writing has concerned itself with plumbing the reason for this delay, the resistant factors which have inhibited revolutionary growth.

Armah's first encounter with post-colonial ennui was his visit in 1963 to Algeria where he worked as a translator on the weekly *Révolution Africaine*. In the early 1960s Algeria was a base for various struggling nationalist movements, and a magnet for many whose disaffection with Western society sought relief in a feasible alternative. After an eight-year struggle against the French, it had in 1962 achieved a hard-won independence under the socialist government of Ben Bella. The official programme of the FLN (Front de Libération Nationale) seemed to offer the prospect of an economy firmly rooted in the concerted strength of the peasantry. In practice, things worked out somewhat differently. The doleful opening of Armah's third novel, *Why Are We So Blest?*, which is partly set in Algiers, records the reality he discovered. In preference to their declared manifesto the government had opted for a free economy in co-operation with the former masters. Half of the Civil Service was still French, and the French military presence, scheduled to terminate at the end of that year, had been extended by the expedient of delegating French officers to the Algerian army. In the South the position was worse. The Saharan mineral rights, which had duly been ceded to the national government in the previous year, had promptly been leased back to French companies. Moreover the Organisation de l'Armée Secrète (OAS), a terrorist organization formed by white settlers to defend their interests, continued to harass the isolated settlements of the Saharan zone, with the result that the whole area was at the mercy of marauding European thugs.

It was hardly a prospect likely to rejoice the heart of an intellectual fired with the hope of a New Jerusalem, but discovering instead the mutilated veterans, heroes of the recent struggle, hanging around the streets importuning pedestrians for an odd dinar. One cannot, I think, fully comprehend the way Armah chose to interpret the situation unless one bears in mind the way his thinking was structured by a reading of one particular theorist, the Martinican psychiatrist and revolutionary, Frantz Fanon.

Fanon and the Theory of Neo-Colonialism

In an article published soon afterwards in *Présence Africaine*, Armah concluded 'the one theorist who has worked out consistent formulations concerning . . . a revolutionary restructuring of African society is Frantz Fanon'.[11] Prior to his death in 1961, Fanon himself had worked as a psychiatrist in various hospitals in the Algerian war zone. The works he published at that time – *L'an cinq de la révolution algérienne*[12] and *Les Damnés de la terre*[13] – provide us with a very distinctive view of social motivation. Through a fusion of clinical observation and historical perspicacity, he develops certain themes concerning the mind of a colonized people. Briefly stated, the major conjectural position is this: that after decades of domination the natives have developed massive inferiority feelings which manifest themselves in an acute dependency on their masters, a state which can only be redeemed by a decisive act of war. Violence not only emancipates them from foreign control; it also, more crucially, helps them to emancipate themselves from abject awe in the face of the industrialized world, thus enabling them to rise to a pitch of equality.

Dying as he did before the end of the war, Fanon never experienced the frustration of these hopes under the Bella government, which was, incidentally, toppled by an army coup shortly before Armah's visit. Yet, paradoxically, his theories provide a means of understanding not only the success of the war, but also the subsequent betrayal. Clearly a war of independence, however protracted, was not sufficient to breach those ties of symbiotic growth which held Algeria to metropolitan France. The sense of dependency was still firmly in place. As the historian Arslan Humbaraci puts it: 'from a revolutionary point of view, French influence after independence inhibited radical social and economic policies'.[14]

Armah's disaffection with the aftermath of independence comes out very strongly in his *Présence Africaine* article, in which he wrote: 'as the Algerian revolutionaries have so sarcastically noted, the African politicians love flashy scenes and high-falutin' words. That is only a partial exploration. More important is the historical fact that in a very radical sense the nationalist leaders of Africa have found themselves sucked into the role of hypocrites, actors involved in a make-believe situation.'[15] These feelings help us to understand the way that he reacted to the Ghanaian situation on his return in 1964. Here again, revolutionary fervour had guttered into political betrayal. Despite its international reputation the Nkrumah regime had dwindled internally to a corrupt cabal. Misled by sycophantic lieutenants, the President had let the country drift further and further into debt. Personal liberties were severely eroded. J. B. Danquah, the scholar and Opposition leader, had died in gaol. Others were in exile. In personal terms Armah's return to his homeland was disappointing. He attempted to find his way through a journalistic career, but, finding the country's newspaper editors unappreciative of his challenging approach to public issues, was forced to abandon the possibility of communicating his vision thus directly. He took to teaching, worked briefly as a Research Fellow at the university, and, more importantly, began writing in earnest. In February 1966, the regime was ousted by a brief military action, and a committee of army officers took over nominally so as to put the economy to rights, in practice in the name of the exiled Opposition leadership which soon came to power. To the Western world this sounded like liberation. But to men of Armah's persuasion it was the very opposite. For, despite Nkrumah's later vagaries, he remained in memory the leader with the popular touch. After his demise, nothing was left but a return to the mildness of 1940s politics, the leadership of the stooges who had preceded him in the nationalist movement, the 'jokers' of *The Beautyful Ones.*

Armah's first two novels are set in Ghana immediately before the 1966 coup d'état. It is therefore fair to say that the desolation of those days left a marked impression on his imagination. But it would be wrong to interpret these books simply on the level of an evocation of despair. They dig much deeper, probing through mere disenchantment towards something closer to analysis. The characters in both of these books, with the exception of their persecuted protagonists, give the impression of being in the grip of a covetous mania, an engrossing hunger for material possessions which prevents them from attending to deeper spiritual needs. For example, it is the mother's desire for the bright things of the white man compared to the Melanesian 'cargo cult', in *Fragments*, which prevents her from appreciating her son's artistic dedication. The man's

family in *The Beautyful Ones* too are so desperate to compete in the
rat-race that they are blind to the considerations which inhibit him from
collaborating in Koomson's boat-buying scheme. It is this lust for
wealth, specifically seen as a kind of material dependence on the capitalist
West, which undermines the solidarity of the people and leads to
sterility.

Clearly what Armah is doing in these books is to explain the cultural
resistance which has led to what he sees as his country's failure. Once
again, the features of this aetiology point to a source in Fanon. Indeed
Fanon himself had visited Ghana a few years previously and had come to
very similar conclusions. In 1960 under the pretext of securing supply
routes for the guerrillas from the South, he had been given the somewhat
spurious appointment of ambassador of the provisional Algerian
Government to Ghana. Arriving in Accra he had experienced a shock
very similar to Armah's. The political élite of the country, which had
been so loud from afar in their cries of fraternity, had apparently given
themselves up to an orgy of spending. He was not impressed. In Armah's
own words 'analysing (mainly from his vantage point in Accra) the antics
of the post-Independence African leadership, he instantly and emphatically refused to be taken in by all the show. He knew all along that all the
slogans and all the pomp and all the torrents of words were at bottom only
an illusionist's art, and he said so.'[16] According to David Caute in his
study of Fanon, it was this discovery which jolted him into formulating
his famous theory of neo-colonialism which has had so profound an effect
on the thinking of so many African writers.[17]

The theory, expounded in *Les Damnés de la terre*, has its roots in the
notion of dependency expanded in Fanon's earlier books. The difference
is that it extends the analysis to explain the failure of nerve evinced by the
governments of so many new nations after Independence. What is it that
keeps them in a state of humiliating reliance on Western aid? Why do the
educated classes of developing nations spend so much time demanding
the crumbs of materialistic prestige to be snatched from Europe, and so
little developing local resources such as agriculture? The answer,
suggests Fanon, is that the governing class of such countries has for so
long left the responsibility of its decisions to others that it is now deprived
of the capacity to take any constructive initiative 'since it implies a
minimum of risk'.[18] The failure is one of imagination. The people have
lost the ability to improvise since they no longer possess the necessary
confidence in the creative potential of their own culture.

It would be an exaggeration to claim that Armah's understanding of his
people's dilemma is determined by his reading of Fanon. What is certain,
however, is that the theory of neo-colonialism supplies a way of looking at

the perplexity of the élites of the Third World which can bind fragmentary insights into a coherent and compelling whole. Above all, it provides an historical explanation for present failure, and hence connects current manifestations to an embracing world-view. The pertinence of this to Armah can be seen when we recognize that his books have increasingly concerned themselves with questions which are ultimately historical in nature. Beginning with his first two books he has evoked the degradation of his people in such a way as to beg the question of its cause. This would seem to have led him to alter his line of approach so that in *Two Thousand Seasons*, for instance, he has forsaken documentary for the wider vistas of historical chronicle. Only thus perhaps can he come to terms with the problems posed in the earlier works.

For many years now Armah has worked outside Ghana, to which he is an infrequent visitor. He has been a translator in Paris, and a lecturer in creative writing in Tanzania, and more recently in Lesotho. He strongly denies that this represents any form of exile. Nevertheless, *The Beautyful Ones* and *Fragments* both give the impression of having been written under the immediate impact of social obloquy and misunderstanding, of needs that find relief in a brittle satire. Latterly, these pressures having apparently abated, Armah has seen fit to expose his preoccupations to a broader perspective. In *Why Are We So Blest?* the breadth is geographical, the self-communing of its two African protagonists exploring an international context. In *Two Thousand Seasons* the breadth is both geographical and historical, a vast slice of human history serving to illuminate that process of imaginative enslavement that has become this writer's overriding obsession.

Style and Symbol

Despite this technical development there are certain factors which remain remarkably consistent in Armah's manner of writing. He is one of the few contemporary writers to whom one can consistently apply one of the tests of true merit: examine any page, any paragraph of his work and you will find the style and sensibility completely characteristic of him. Not only, for example, could one emphatically affirm that no other writer could have achieved a book like *The Beautyful Ones Are Not Yet Born*. The same is true of any one of its paragraphs. There is something about the shape of each sentence, the resonance of the words as they echo in the head, that brands each verbal and mental movement as triumphantly Armah's own.

Perhaps because of his vivid historical sense, Armah's style seems closely attuned to a particular way of registering the passage of time. Time moves not in the rigorous chronological progression from one instant or period to the next invoked by the academic historian, but in a remorseless, almost cyclical pattern, reminiscent of the traditional notion of historical experience noted by Emmanuel Obiechina:

> The past is never remote from the present but is frequently a back extension as well as a reinforcement of the present, a manner of elucidating contemporaneous experience as well as a validation of such experience. There is a deep and abiding interest in history, not as a dead substance of remote antiquity, but as an accumulation of human achievement, a testimony of human ingenuity and will reaching down to ancestral roots.[19]

Obiechina goes on to say that he regards this way of perceiving time as being characteristic of novels set in the rural environment, whereas writers who concentrate on urban situations have to pace their narratives with a much more fleeting rhythm. It is Armah's achievement that all his works, whether grittily urban like *The Beautyful Ones* or, like *Two Thousand Seasons*, predominantly rural, evoke very much the same sense of continuity. There is a liberation from literal time processes which gives his prose an almost disembodied feel, highly distinctive in his haunting flow:

> Each thing that goes away returns and nothing in the end is lost. The great friend throws all things apart and brings all things together again. That is the way everything goes and turns round. That is how all living things come back after long absences, and in the whole great world all things are living things. All that goes returns. He will return.[20]

Here, in the moving opening section of *Fragments*, Naana, the frail and blind grandmother, is talking about the expected return of Baako, her grandson, from his studies in America. For her this is no single episode, but part of a huge cycle of death and rebirth, sanctified by the gods, which is slowly but inexorably carrying her towards her grave. In order to achieve a sense of continuous flux, Armah has recourse to three very individual devices. First, the whole paragraph is stated in the present tense as if Naana were holding the whole course of history in her steady, unshifting gaze. Then there is the consistent use of repetition, the shape and cadence of each sentence recalling the last in a way suggestive of incantation. Lastly, one notices how much of the weight of the syntax is thrown onto the nouns, consigning the verbs to a comparatively innocuous function: 'in the whole great world all things are living things'. Each substantive, heavily laden with adjectives, serves to fix the abstract sense of the passage, while the verbs refuse to pin these significances down to any one instant or place.

At points such as this Armah's sense of timelessness surfaces so that we can examine the way that it affects his style in some detail. Normally, however, it is far from explicit, remaining as an element in the background of which we are scarcely aware. Yet it is always there informing the way in which even the most localized of passages is rendered.

> The reproach of loved ones comes kindly when it comes in silence. Even when this silence is filled with the consciousness of resentment, there is always the hope that they understand whatever vague little wishes there are to understand, as if one could forever keep up the pretense that the difference between the failures and the hard heroes of the dream is only a matter of time. Time in which to leap across yards made up of the mud of days of rain; to jump over wide gutters with only a trickle of drying urine at the bottom and so many clusters of cigarette pieces wet and pinched in where they have left the still unsatisfied lips of the sucker. Time to sail with a beautiful smoothness in the sweet direction of the gleam, carrying with easy strength every one of the loved ones; time to change the silent curses of resentful loved ones and the deeper silent questions of those in whom pain and disappointment have killed every other emotion, time to change all this into the long unforced laughter of tired travellers home at last.[21]

In this passage, from the fifth chapter of *The Beautyful Ones*, the novelist is describing the 'man's' return after a day at the office. For the 'man' this daily experience he must endure is one of perennial guilt for the squalid conditions in which his professional failure has forced his family to live, for the carefully nurtured hopes he has laid waste through his stubborn refusal to take the lazy road to success. Because the experience is a daily one, constantly anticipated in dread, Armah employs just those stylistic features noted in the previous passage: the present tense to evoke the immediate horror of remorse; the repetition; the long line of nouns and epithets only occasionally relieved by a verb. A close scrutiny also reveals various ways in which the number of verbs has been reduced by converting them into nouns. For instance, 'the sucker', 'the loved ones' are in effect nominalizations of verbs which, because they are framed grammatically in this way, deprive the verb of its tense, and thus refrain from fixing the action in any one moment of time. It is this which produces the 'drugged or somnambulistic tempo' of which Gerald Moore speaks,[22] and vividly conveys the sensation of a man bound on a wheel of fire from which there is no escaping.

Another feature of Armah's writing much flaunted by the critics is his constant and systematic reliance on symbolism. A more detailed treatment will have to wait for the chapters on individual novels. Suffice it here to note that there are certain symbols which transcend the divisions between the books, recurring in such a way as to amount to motifs pervading the whole of Armah's writing. The most obvious of these is the stream which surfaces in the third chapter of *The Beautyful Ones* and, in its meandering, imperilled progress to the sea, runs through most of the novels to date. Wherever it occurs the connotation would seem to be of an indigenous, prehistoric sense of integrity attempting to force its way through the accumulated moral pollution of the centuries. It is hence integrally connected with that other image-cluster so often mentioned, the various embodiments of filth, from the faeces and rotting refuse of *The Beautyful Ones* to the clotted sand which impedes the 'springwater' in *Two Thousand Seasons*.

Thus we can see that, right at the imagistic heart of these books there is this constant visualization of a conflict essential to Armah's vision of history: the struggle between the native genius of a people trying to assert its cultural integrity, and the forces, usually internalized, which would divert it into alien channels. The tension is most acute in the contemporary scene, where the tempting goods of the Western world seem illuminated by the neon 'gleam' of commercialized romance. But the roots lie way back in the abysses of history, in a confrontation it has been Armah's trenchant purpose to examine.

REFERENCES AND NOTES

1. See, for example, Jonathan Kariara in *Zuka* (Nairobi), no. 4 (December 1969), pp. 57–8.
2. Ayi Kwei Armah, *The Beautyful Ones Are Not Yet Born* (Boston: Houghton Mifflin, 1968; London: Heinemann Educational Books, 1969). Translated into Swahili as *Wema Hawajazaliwa* (Nairobi: Heinemann (East Africa), 1976).
3. Arthur Ravenscroft, 'Novels of disillusion', *Journal of Commonwealth Literature* no. 6 (January 1969), pp. 120–37.
4. Emmanuel Obiechina, review in *Okike* (Nigeria, Nsukka) (April 1971), p. 52.
5. Jonathan Kariara, *op. cit.*
6. See, for instance, Gerald Moore, 'Armah's second novel', *Journal of Commonwealth Literature*, vol. ix, no. 1 (August 1974), p. 71.
7. Ioan Davies, *African Trade Unions* (Harmondsworth: Penguin Books, 1966), p. 81.
8. At Saltpont in June 1949. See Basil Davidson, *Black Star* (London: Allen Lane, Penguin Books, 1973), p. 68.
9. David Apter, *Ghana in Transition*, 2nd edn (Princeton: Princeton University Press, 1972), p. 127.
10. Ayi Kwei Armah, *Why Are We So Blest?* (New York: Doubleday, 1972; London: Heinemann Educational Books, 1974; Nairobi: East African Publishing House, 1974), pp. 98–103. Page reference is to Heinemann edition.
11. Ayi Kwei Armah, 'African socialism: utopian or scientific', *Présence Africaine* (Paris), no. 64 (1967), p. 29.
12. Frantz Fanon, *L'an cinq de la révolution algérienne* (Paris: Maspero, 1959).
13. Frantz Fanon, *Les Damnés de la terre* (Paris: Maspero, 1961).
14. Arslan Humbaraci, *Algeria, a Revolution that Failed* (London: Pall Mall, 1966), p. 205.

15. Ayi Kwei Armah, 'African socialism: utopian or scientific', *op. cit.*, p. 28.

16. *Ibid.*, p. 29.

17. David Caute, *Fanon* (Glasgow: Collins, 1970), pp. 60–1.

18. Frantz Fanon, *The Wretched of the East* (Harmondsworth: Penguin Books, 1967), p. 124.

19. Emmanuel Obiechina, *Culture, Tradition and Society in the West African Novel* (Cambridge: Cambridge University Press, 1975), p. 133.

20. Ayi Kwei Armah, *Fragments* (Boston: Houghton Mifflin, 1970; London: Heinemann Educational Books, 1974; Nairobi: East African Publishing House, 1974), p. 1.

21. Ayi Kwei Armah, *The Beautyful Ones Are Not Yet Born* (London: Heinemann Educational Books, 1969), p. 46.

22. Gerald Moore, *op. cit.*, p. 70.

2 *The Beautyful Ones Are Not Yet Born*

▼▼▼▼▼▼▼▼▼▼▼▼▼▼▼▼▼▼▼▼▼▼▼▼▼▼▼▼▼▼

*T*HE *Beautyful Ones Are Not Yet Born*[1] was the first novel which Armah published. Partly for that reason, and partly because of the uncompromising stand it takes on certain aspects of Ghana's national life, it has attracted considerably more critical attention than his subsequent books. Though overwhelmingly complimentary to Armah's talent, much of this has concentrated rather narrowly on a few contentious areas of discussion. His fearless castigation of contemporary corruption, for instance, has been emphasized at the expense of his compassionate sense of human frailty. His wholesale disgust at the antics of African politicians has been noticed by everybody; few have noted the way in which this is portrayed as part of a much larger pattern of betrayal. Nobody appears to have savoured his droll, ashen humour. For Eldred Jones 'the dominating mood of the novel is one of hopeless despair';[2] E. N. Obiechina talks of its 'rigid moral positions';[3] Molly Mahood concludes that 'the dominating mood of the novel is one of almost total disillusionment'.[4] Behind many of these opinions one can discern the shadow of a defensive posture. Confronted with a work so destructive of patriotic complacency, many critics have tended to confuse the charge of treason with that of artistic deficiency. Hence Armah comes to be saddled with strictures which are essentially political rather than artistic in nature. His misfortune in this regard is similar to another writer from the Third World: the Trinidadian novelist, V. S. Naipaul. In both, a determination to see things straight has been taken as a kind of obsessive and twisted acidity. The charge is distinctly unfair to both of them.

The following is typical of one kind of misunderstanding:

As for dragging in Nkrumah and some of the pointed criticisms against this regime, one must regard them as a result of an error of judgment on the part of the novelist. The whole thing is capable of stoking up so much unnecessary controversy. The events surrounding Nkrumah's reign and overthrow in Ghana are too complex and open to diverse interpretations to be safely handled in this kind of fiction. On the level of parable, it might pass but on the particularized level of fact, it raises numerous weighty questions which, given the limitations of the fictional medium, cannot be adequately dealt with. Maybe Armah has not heard of the word 'neocolonialism' or how it operates on the African man and on the African political destiny. Maybe he underrates what has been called 'the colonialism of the mind'.[5]

The limitations imputed to the fictional medium here are of the critic's own making. Insisting on interpreting the book on the level of parable, he denies Armah any insight into the opaque recesses of motivation, and thus construes his attitudes to the élite as one of arrant condemnation. This prevents him from recognizing the forceful mitigating factors sketched out in the novel, with the result that he attempts to correct Armah by indicating the absence of what are, in fact, his salient themes: 'neocolonialism' and 'the colonialism of the mind'.

The protagonist of *The Beautyful Ones*, called simply 'the man' throughout, is a down-at-heel Morse operator in the employ of the Ghana Railway Corporation at Takoradi. The term by which he is designated suggests both his social obscurity and, partially, his representative quality. For, caught in the trap of a mundane and unremunerative occupation, he is subject to all those petty, debilitating pressures from which a more dignified status might have exempted him. His work is dull and unrewarding. His family, frustrated by poverty and deferred expectations, are pinched and resentful. Mournfully he drags himself through each working day with little to anticipate in the evening but the accusing eyes of his wife and children, their nagging envy of those whose financial situation is happier.

The man has two redeeming qualities. The first is his acute and sensitive intelligence. For the man did not choose this mode of existence: forced to forgo his early ambitions because of an amorous misadventure, he is continually tortured by thoughts of the future he might have had, the gap that has widened between him and those of his less able contemporaries who have achieved eminence. His intelligence, however, is less a matter of sheer ability than of the moral focus which he brings to bear both on his own life and on those of his countrymen. His suffering is heightened by an awareness of lost opportunities, political betrayal and cultural dislocation. The other quality is his stubborn refusal to compromise on basic principles, an integrity of intention which exposes him to general obloquy and familial contempt. Of all the characters in the novel he is virtually alone in his decision to put into practice the official Party ideals of 'hard work and honesty and integrity' (p. 95).

His difficulties are only increased by the fact that his job confronts him with numerous opportunities to improve his lot by accepting bribes. In the third chapter an Ashanti timber contractor visits the office while the man is doing overtime and attempts to bribe him into providing the wagon space necessary for transporting his rapidly degenerating logs from a neglected siding in the forest. The sadly knowing attitude which the man takes to this proposal, and his wife's weary impatience when she learns of his refusal to comply, tell us that this is not the first time that he has refused the fruits of graft and greed. Despite this, the man's attitude lacks any tincture of self-righteousness. He is very far from a prig. His sense of propriety in this matter is governed, not by a burning indignation at the cupidity of others, but by a straightforward insistence on taking prescribed procedures literally. As he comments to his exasperated wife, 'it wasn't even necessary' (p. 43). His remark says as much about the inefficiency of the organization for which he works in not providing the contractor with his allocation as it does about the reputation for corruptibility that invited the bribe.

His abstinence is made all the harder by the prospect of Koomson, an old school friend, successfully scaling the upward path towards the giddy heights of power. Koomson's success is the result of moral laxity and an ability to spot the main chance. From political involvement with the dockers in the 1950s he has proceeded through the Ideological Institute at Winneba, the instant breeding ground for party hacks, to the ultimate accolade of a plum government appointment. In the bloated language of bureaucratic deference he is now 'His Excellency Joseph Koomson, Minister Plenipotentiary, Member of the Presidential Commission, Hero of Socialist Labor' (p. 56). He now lives in one of the brasher residential estates that previously accommodated the envied colonizer. His coarse docker's accent is thinly disguised by an assumed hauteur. His wife bedecked with imported finery, his sister-in-law studying in England for a higher course (albeit in sewing), his life is irradiated by that dazzling gleam the man's own so conspicuously lacks. Sailing along in a chauffeured Mercedes Benz, he is a living reproach for what the man's wife interprets as her husband's fundamental lack of initiative.

It is Koomson rather than the man who is seen to epitomize the moral outlook of the nation, for, despite his wealth and prestige, Koomson's ideals correspond to the triumphant average. His mind perennially occupied with money-making schemes, he glories in the kudos of his office with no apparent sense of responsibility towards those to whom he owes it. Yet, despite his sense of exclusiveness, he is essentially a creature of the times; his vapid materialism acts as an intense focus of the cravings of a nation obsessively bent on the pillage of its newly acquired spoils. When he condescends to visit the man's home, the latter's family hang on his every word. Yet all he has to offer are cheap jokes at the expense of the intelligentsia, together with an avowed propensity for alcohol, preferably imported. Materially opulent, he is morally bankrupt, a complete contradiction of everything for which the Party officially stands. However, it is Koomson whom the people envy, not the man, a preference which tells us much about the state of the national consciousness. To many reviewers, the portrait of Koomson has seemed simply a means of slandering the leadership. To a certain extent this is true, but it is balanced by the fact that his propensities are shared by many of the humbler characters, whose capacity to express them is, however, limited. The bus conductor in the opening chapter who sniffs at an old cedi note (p. 3); the allocations clerk who eventually accepts the contractor's bribe (p. 107); the policeman who hurries a lorry through his check-point for a consideration (pp. 182–3): all of these are victims along with Koomson of a common ailment, further illustrated by the graffiti the man finds scrawled on the walls of the office latrine:

MONEY SWEET. PASS ALL
To the left there are others, a bit harder to make out at first.
WHO BORN FOOL
SOCIALISM CHOP MAKE I CHOP
CONTREY BROKE. (p. 106)

Koomson is merely distinguished by his success.

There is in all this desolation just one person to whom the man feels that he can turn for some sort of consolation: another friend, Teacher. Teacher shares a common viewpoint with the man; his means of expressing it is, however, different. The one major tendency they have in common is a marked preference for austerity: when the man goes to see him, he finds Teacher stretched naked in a stark room listening to Congo music on the radio. Yet for Teacher this austerity is the outward form of an inner dedication which is only partly moral. He has pared himself to the minimum in the service of a contemplative ideal, and, at least potentially, of the articulation of intuited truth. His autobiographical references suggest an intellectual provenance: part-mystic, part-writer, part-preacher. If the man is Everyman, beset with temporal concerns, then Teacher is an artist with an artist's special plea to be heard. Yet, as with many true artists, he is condemned to cry in the wilderness. Commenting on the lovely sadness of the lyrics he has been listening to on his radio, he contrasts his own attitude to such song-writers as 'poets who have failed' to the inevitable general verdict that, on the other hand, 'poets are bandleaders who have failed' (p. 52). The distinction tells us much about the estimation in which art is currently held: artists, along with everybody else, are judged by the size of their wallets rather than the truth of their vision.

Teacher's social isolation is mirrored by his personal circumstances. Unmarried, he remains uncluttered by the demands of 'the loved ones'. Because of this he appears on the surface to possess greater self-sufficiency than the man, a calm poise his friend mistakes for serenity. In effect, however, Teacher has only solved his moral problems by simplifying them. He has deliberately contrived his situation so that his honesty hurts no one but himself. In the last resort there is too little parity between his position and the man's for him to be able to offer viable advice. Moreover, though superficially composed, he gradually reveals to us much the same bewilderment as the man, towards whom his attitude vacillates between affectionate contempt and sneaking admiration.

Ultimately the man is subdued by the realization that he faces his dilemma alone. He is stuck with an ethical fastidiousness which in his position is completely inappropriate. He can only steer a devious course between half-hearted, dryly witty protest and tactful complicity. His problems come to a head when Koomson, wishing to purchase an expensive fishing vessel for his own profit, yet fearful of the reaction this might provoke among his eagle-eyed enemies, proposes to register the boat in the man's name. Under the man's remorseless questioning he admits that no advantage will accrue to the technical owners under this arrangement except a meagre supply of fish. For the man's family, however, the deal seems to open out receding vistas of possible gain, and a magic contact with the admired world of ostentatious living. The man's misgivings are quashed by his family, who persuade him to pursue the matter. Eventually, when documents are produced, he baulks the issue. He allows his wife to sign in his stead (p. 150).

Koomson elicits from the man a complex attitude which in some ways distils his predicament. At bottom he knows his friend's kind of success to be detestable. He is under no illusions as to his friend's ability, or his morality. Yet, faced with the wearying demands of his family and the plain prospect of his own failure, it is hard for him to sustain his contempt with any conviction. He is for ever haunted by the possibility that his scruples are nothing but a cover for weakness, for his lack of the sort of ruthless dexterity Koomson too obviously displays:

> I am asking myself what is wrong with me. Do I have some part missing? Teacher, this Koomson was my own classmate. My classmate, Teacher, my classmate. So tell me, what is wrong with me? (p. 57)

The man contemplates Koomson's strength from a position of weakness. In the closing chapters, however, their roles are cataclysmally reversed. Overhearing at the office the news of the February coup, the man's response is glum:

> What, after all, could it mean? One man, with the help of people who loved him and believed in him, had arrived at power and used it for

himself. Now other men, with the help of guns, had come to this same power. (p. 157)

Yet for him personally the change of government proves to have repercussions, since, arriving back at the house, he discovers Koomson cowering in the bedroom in fear of his life. The tables have turned; the exploiters have now become the pursued. Initially this has the effect of intensifying the man's old contempt. He nevertheless decides to help his old classmate, less perhaps out of any residual loyalty than the same lustreless sense of moral obligation as had prevented him taking bribes. Paradoxically his intervention leads him straight into the kind of compromise he has so far avoided since, after rescuing Koomson from imminent arrest and guiding him to the point on the beach where the boat lies anchored, he finds their way blocked by the nightwatchman, who, recognizing Koomson, holds out for a bribe. In the urgency of the moment, the man lends his support:

> The boatman hesitated. But the man turned to him and said, 'Give it to him, if there's another one.' (p. 176)

Once launched, the boat carries them westwards towards Abidjan. After a cursory farewell, the man dives off into the sea, leaving Koomson to sail on towards the Ivory Coast and freedom. As he makes his way along the coastal road back to Takoradi he spots a policeman, an agent now of the new, officially purged, regime, accepting a bribe from a lorry driver, whose vehicle bears the quaint motto of the novel's title. Confirmed in pessimism, the man plods on. It is still uncertain who is the fool.

The overall effect of the novel is to fix a sense of a whole nation labouring under a corrosive malaise. Though many of the sharpest barbs in the book are reserved for Koomson and his kind, Koomson's attitudes, as we have seen, act merely as a distillation of the aspirations of his countrymen. The sickness afflicts all levels of society from the humblest office cleaner to the most pampered government minister. Furthermore, to confine Armah's analysis to certainly palpably corrupt practices such as bribery is to confine his point and hence to anaesthetize it. Men take bribes because they are subjected to certain kinds of social pressure; in other societies, under different conditions the compelling need would not arise. Armah's method digs way beneath his superficial satire; it becomes a means of exposing the eddies of disturbance below the manifestly rotten surface.

What are the symptoms of this national illness? Fundamentally it appears to betray itself as an almost obsessive self-distrust, a determination to dismiss anything of local inspiration while admiring everything which originates from abroad. Estella Koomson is typical in her protestation against locally manufactured spirits: 'Really, the only good drinks are European drinks. These make you ill' (p. 132). The same preference afflicts all aspects of the nation's life style. The denizens of the Senior Service residential estate inflict incredible injuries on their names so as to force them into the most convincing double-barrelled European equivalents. The results are predictably grotesque:

> In the forest of white men's names, there were the signs that said almost aloud: here lives a black imitator. MILLS-HAYFORD ... PLANGE-BANNERMAN ... ATTOH-WHITE ... KUNTU-BLANKSON. Others that must have been keeping the white neighbors laughing even harder in their homes. ACROMOND ... what Ghanaian name could that have been in the beginning, before its Civil Servant owner rushed to civilize it, giving it something like the sound of a master name. (p. 126)

One occupant, in a manner typical of Ghanaian English, has even fused 'been-to' with the common suffix '-ful' (as in 'fridgeful') to produce the ultimately snobbish BINFUL.[6] Such cultural acrobatics are not confined to the élite. The overtime clerk at the Railway Administration Building screws his face into fantastic distortions so as to achieve the pellucid tones of received English pronunciation. The result is a parody of an Oxbridge accent that the man can hardly understand (pp. 24–5).

The seductive allure of all things foreign and exotic is suggested throughout the book by references to 'the gleam', a phenomenon which recurs with almost symbolic consistency to denote the sort of luxury which is beyond the reach of most Ghanaians. Implicitly contrasted with the honest sunlight heralded by 'the bringer' in Teacher's version of Plato's myth of the cave (pp. 79–80), 'the gleam' invariably evokes the sulphur brilliance of artificial light in tropical darkness, the glow of tall buildings bathed in the caress of floodlight, the sharp glitter of chrome caught in a cross-beam. It is embodied throughout the book by the gleaming façade of the Atlantic Hotel staring out to sea and attracting to itself and its habitués the envy of those who will never afford its pleasures. It plays lovingly on the imported objects of the Koomsons' living-room, luminous with glass and polished metal:

> It was amazing how much light there was in a place like this. It glinted off every object in the room. Next to each ashtray there were two shiny things: a silver box and a small toy-like pistol. The man wondered what the pistols were for. Light came off the marble tops of the little side tables. (pp. 145–6)

'The gleam' is, as Margaret Folarin has demonstrated, substantially connected with a wider imagery of light and shadow.[7] It also has its relevance to the various ways in which the characters in the book conceive of hygiene. Habitually 'cleanliness' is ascribed to those aspects of life which approximate most closely to the European. An early instance is Teacher's memory of the attraction he felt in childhood for the silt-free water which coursed down from the ridge:

> And the water coming down from the hills was always clean, like unused water, or like water used by ghosts without flesh. (p. 67)

Cleanliness is always seen as a release from familiar squalor, a glamorous mode of escape from cloying social circumstances. As such, it is the counterpoise to all those images of excrement and putrefaction in which the novel is so rich. The means of escape is through social, rather than moral, eminence. Talking of the extravagant existence she so much envies in Estella Koomson, Oyo, the man's hard-bitten wife, puts the difference between them thus: 'It is nice. It is clean, the life Estella is getting.' The man's retort is characteristically sardonic: 'Some of that kind of cleanliness has more rottenness in it than the slime at the bottom of a garbage dump' (p. 44). His own preferences in the matter are graphically illustrated during his conversation with the timber contractor. When, tempting him, the business man asks, 'What do you drink?', the man answers emphatically, 'Water' (p. 30). Our reaction here is to sense that the man is practically alone in his appreciation of what it might be to be truly clean.

The man's insight, however, remains on the level of intermittent perception; in practice, even in volition, it is hard for him to sustain it. Many critical accounts of the book depend on our seeing the man as its moral linchpin, a role which, in the last resort, he is incapable of fulfilling. For the man is almost as blighted as his countrymen; his sole redeeming feature is that, unlike the rest, he recognizes his lesions. In his dream sequence in Chapter 8, he feels himself vainly trudging along an arc-lit road, pulled by the merging 'gleam' of the towers of Legon and the Atlantic-Caprice (p. 100). It is an attraction which, in his sager moments, he knows to be a weakness. Yet there are other times when he is prepared to see in all this envy the possibility of a creative force:

> Having the whiteness of stolen bungalows and the shine of stolen cars flowing past him, he could think of reasons, of the probability that without the belittling power of things like these we would all continue to sit underneath old trees and weave palm wine dreams of beauty and happiness in our amazed heads. And so the gleam of all this property would have the power to make us work harder, would come between ourselves and our desires for rest, so that through wanting the things our own souls crave we would end up moving a whole people forward. (p. 94)

Sitting in Koomson's living-room, drinking in the splendour and the light, the man's head echoes with a harrowing refrain: 'For the little children' (p. 145). It is a call which urges the necessity of investing, however corruptly, in the future, the futility of a merely specious restraint. At moments like these Koomson's life comes to seem endowed with a kind of remorseless logic. As the man confesses to Teacher:

> I only wish I could speak with your contempt for what goes on. But I do not know whether it is envy that makes me hate what I see. I am not even sure that I hate it, Teacher. (p. 92)

Speculations of this sort have the effect of compounding the man's confusion with a stinging guilt. Trapped between social obligation and ethical scrupulosity, his cherished principles come to wear the face of indecisiveness, or, worse, bigotry. When he confides in Teacher his refusal to take the bribe, the latter brands him 'murderer' (p. 53). It is an indictment which echoes his own feelings, for a few pages earlier we read:

> How could he, when all around him the whole world never tired of saying there were only two types of men who took refuge in honesty – the cowards and the fools? Very often these days he was burdened with the hopeless, impotent feeling that he was not just one of these, but a hopeless combination of the two. Thoughts and images rose of the lonely man trapped at a bar, who does not drink but feels far more confused than all the masquerading drinkers, and when the images came closer to merge with his own self, he was the careful man refusing to gamble with his life, and therefore feeling the keen-eyed reproach of those closest to himself. And all the time the eyes that could never be avoided just stared steadily and made it terrifyingly plain that in these times honesty could only be a social vice, for the one who chose to indulge in it nothing but a very hostile form of selfishness, a very perverse selfishness. (pp. 51–2)

Incapacitated by such self-knowledge, the man is completely disqualified from the role of judge sometimes allotted to him. In the occasionally Christian sensibility of this novel the act of judgement comes to seem the ultimate arrogance. A polemical aside in Chapter 6 dismisses the presumption of legal judges who dispatch young men to prison for smoking the 'wee' (marijuana) that they themselves have never dared even to taste (p. 70). The man shares something of these authorial misgivings. Counterbalancing his evident sense of his people's depravity is a strong and compassionate sense of the mitigating forces which have driven men and women to sacrifice their scruples for the mere means to live. His squibs of wit at the expense of others are reserved for those who, like Koomson, have flourished at the expense of their fellow men.

Otherwise, he is far too deeply preoccupied with working at his own problems to spare casual energy for the denigration of those whose painful plight he shares.

The man's position in this regard is made quite plain when we first encounter him journeying to work at the beginning of the book. As the bus shudders to a halt in the growing dawn the passengers file out leaving the conductor, as he thinks, alone. Settling himself on the hard step to examine the day's takings, he is just sniffing ecstatically at the aroma of an old cedi note, when his attention is alerted by a remaining passenger slumped in the back seat, apparently watching him. It is the man:

> A pair of wide open, staring eyes met his. The man was sitting in the very back of the bus, with his body angled forward so that his chin was resting on the back of the seat in front of him, supported by his hands. The eyes frightened the conductor. Even the mere remembered smell of the cedi was now painful, and the feeling in his armpit had suddenly become very cold. Was this the giver turned watcher already? (pp. 3–4)

Prompted by his own uneasy feelings of remorse the conductor immediately sets the man 'above himself' (p. 5) in a judging position. Nervously he approaches his apparent accuser to conciliate him with a cigarette – 'You see, we can share' (p. 5), when he notices a thin line of spittle extending from the corner of the man's mouth down to the torn plastic of the bus seat. At length the truth strikes home: 'The watcher was no watcher after all, only a sleeper' (p. 5). Automatically the conductor himself assumes a posture of judgement – 'Article of no commercial value! You think the bus belongs to your grandfather?' – (p. 6) upon which the mortified man attempts apologetically to extinguish his slime by rubbing it into the seat cover. It is a gesture of foreboding. The man begins the novel by contributing to his messy environment, just as he finishes it by endorsing an act of bribery. Throughout, his aura of judgement must be taken as an illusion, a projection of the reader's own need for some sort of reassuring moral centre.

The context of the man's confusion can be seen even more clearly in the episode with the timber contractor in Chapter 3. He is just settling into the 'comforting loneliness' of an evening's overtime when the immense bulk of the businessman eases itself through the door. The man's instinctive distrust of ostentation is aroused by the showy kente cloth, the 'too many tufts' of the sandals. Nevertheless he deals with the contractor's proposition with literal fairness, pointing out the anomaly of his position, his inability to accept payment. There is nothing about him of the surly employee, unwilling to put himself out. Yet one retains only a very vague sense of the reason for the man's refusal to comply. Indeed he seems far from clear himself:

'But what is wrong?' the visitor asked again.
'Wrong?'
'Yes my friend. Why do you behave like that?'
'I don't know,' the man said. (p. 31)

In order to appreciate the reasons for the man's perplexity here it is well to bear in mind some of the economic and social factors impinging on the issue. The man is an employee of the railways. The railway system of the Gold Coast was developed during the 1920s as a quick and easy way of exporting the wealth – timber, cocoa, gold – from the hinterland. Takoradi itself exists at the left apex of a communications triangle that takes in the gold-mining towns of Obuasi and Tarkwa as well as the timber capital Kumasi. In the words of Armah's account the railways are there 'to bring Tarkwa gold and Aboso manganese to the waiting Greek ships in the harbor' (p. 21). By assisting in this operation the man is necessarily collaborating in the exploitation. To get the raw materials out quickly can be seen as part of a complicity to ruin the country: it is also, however, the only way of abstracting a few drops of the foreign magnate's profit. But, since these drops are bound to flow straight into the coffers of indigenous exploiters, men such as this Ashanti contractor, the ethical complexities seem endless. The man hardly knows himself which is less forgivable, to take the bribe or to leave it.

Thus throughout the book primary moral impulses are seen to be hedged about with endless qualifications arising from the actual conditions of life inside which they must operate. The man's elemental sense of integrity, for instance, may not be socially determined; the available ways in which it may apply itself certainly are. The man is not, like Sartre's characters, for example, a free agent: he has to be seen, in common with all the other characters, as an expression of his society. To claim, with some critics[8] that the man evinces the sensibility of an expatriate is to denigrate at once him, Ghanaian people in general, and the novel. The man's revulsion, moral and physical, from the squalor in which he must toil is quite characteristic of many who endure such circumstances. His insight may be exceptional, but his sense of shame is absolutely not. Like the young sweeper Bakha in Mulk Raj Anand's novel of Indian life *Untouchable*,[9] he is the product of a long process that has left him and his kind stranded far from hope, from the simple human fulfilment their common sense of dignity teaches them to demand. The man's confusion is but another result of this process.

To put it another way, the man is a victim of history. The historical dimension in the book is a very important aspect of Armah's general vision. It is observable from two angles: the short perspective of recent Ghanaian politics, and the longer perspective of a centuries-old cultural betrayal. The first is explored during an extensive interpolation which takes up the whole of the sixth chapter. The speaker is Teacher, but since at several points in the narrative he appeals to the man to confirm the events described, the impression given is that of a common investigation of shared memories. Without it we would be hard pressed to understand either character's present state of mind. We are shown a society totally conditioned to despair. 'Disillusionment' is strictly impossible, since Teacher and the man grow up with the knowledge that their future is already forfeit, their birthright bartered in advance to the occupants of the 'white men's gleaming bungalows' (p. 66). Up on the ridge succulent mangoes tempt the impish appetite; only in the native township does a whole generation grow into an ingrained awareness that there is, in the phrase borrowed by Ama Atta Aidoo for her volume of stories so similar in mood,[10] 'no sweetness here' (p. 67). The appearance of an indigenous political leadership is received without surprise or enthusiasm, instantly dismissed as yet another turn of a drearily-familiar pattern, since 'they come like men already grown fat and cynical with the eating of centuries of power' (p. 81). The first inkling of Nkrumah's emergence is dismissed likewise; long experience has taught the people to categorize anybody who espouses their cause as another 'new old lawyer, wanting to be white' (p. 84). Only very gradually are they dragged, in the teeth of precious predispositions, towards a belated acceptance of this man as an authentic saviour. Something about the style and simplicity of the man raises the brief flicker of a deceptive hope. Hence, when Nkrumah too eventually fails them, the realization comes not with the bitterness of disenchantment so much as the weary recognition of a long established truth. Thus Nkrumah, who appeared fleetingly to offer an unlooked-for exception, serves ultimately to confirm the overwhelming rule.

Why are the children of the man's generation seen to grow up with such low expectations? The answer is illuminated by the longer historical perspective, which highlights a backdrop of centuries of oppression, a recurrent cycle of despair. Behind the actual details of the plot the deeper pattern is occasionally observable. One instance is when, on receiving Koomson's visit, the man is obliged to shake the minister's hand:

> The man, when he shook hands, was again amazed at the flabby softness of the hand. Ideological hands, the hands of revolutionaries leading their people into bold sacrifices, should these hands not have become even tougher than they were when their owner was hauling loads along the wharf? And yet these were the socialists of Africa, fat, perfumed, soft with the ancestral softness of chiefs who had sold their people and are celestially happy with the fruits of the trade. (p. 131)

The description here forces us to see Koomson as the latest in a long line of indigenous exploiters, beginning with the chiefs who collaborated in the European slave trade and ending with the demagogues of the new Africa. Koomson's ancestry goes back four hundred years. Again, when the man and his wife return the visit, and Koomson hints darkly at the bureaucratic strings which may be pulled to acquire the fishing-boat, the man muses:

> He could have asked if anything was supposed to have changed after all, from the days of chiefs selling their people for the trinkets of Europe. (p. 149)

The 'trinkets' here are identified by implication with the 'small, intricate objects that must have come from foreign lands' lying around Koomson's living-room (p. 146). The procedure is thus seen to be the same in both cases: Koomson, like the slave-dealers, has squandered his people's destiny for the sake of a luxurious triviality.

Thus the social and political corruption of contemporary Ghana are seen to be the legacy of years of moral compromise, a history of duplicity which precedes Independence, precedes perhaps even colonialism itself. The filth is cumulative: it has now piled itself so high that only the penetrating intelligence of the man and Teacher can discern the original wholesomeness that lies somewhere beneath the festering refuse. Seen from an historical viewpoint, the man's isolation is caused by the fact that, together with Teacher, he retains a glimmering, indistinct sense of virtues long since lost to the rest of his society. These virtues are essentially communal ones – the man's vision is nothing if not social – yet, due to the perverting influence of time, the man's espousal of them has the effect of setting him apart from the very people his values are designed to serve.

The historical vision which emerges here is substantially endorsed by the novel's imagery. A very obvious case in point is the much-quoted description at the end of the first chapter of the banister which runs up the stairway in the railway administration building. The passage is a complex one which yields deeper meanings at each reading. It is an example of Armah gradually clarifying his theme through systematic repetition and refinement. As the man turns into the building on his way to work he grasps the stair-rail from which his fingers instantly recoil in disgust at its tacky viscosity, its almost 'organic' feel (p. 11). Examining it, he discovers it to be covered in superimposed layers of polish, paint and grime. Yet there are various cracks in this deep coating through which can be detected the supporting structure of 'a dubious piece of deeply aged brown wood'. At this point, in the first paragraph, it seems as if a contest is being defined between the virginal essence of the wood and the corrupting cosmetic substances which cover it. An historical struggle is implied 'carried on in the silence of long ages' between the vision of 'lunatic seers', those who like the man retain a sense of original purity, and the 'strugglers' with 'deceiving, easy breathing', those who have been seduced by the dazzling allure of artifice. Hence, on its first appearance, the statement 'The wood underneath would win and win till the end of time' reads as a promise of the man's ultimate victory. However, immediately a disconcerting note is sounded: 'it was in the nature of the wood to rot with age'. If, as the description implies, the destructive work of those who handle the rail is supplemented by an inner disintegration, then the whole structure is threatened from within. Thus, when we again encounter the sentence 'the wood would always win' at the very end of the chapter, we are forced to recognize the sinister suggestion that the wood will work its own undoing. A second reading reveals the repeated sentence as a sombre refrain signalling the futility of everything for which the man is striving. History is rotten through and through.

Another instance occurs in Chapter 3. Just before his encounter with the timber contractor the man takes a walk during his lunch break and settles on a concrete slab which has flung itself across the course of a muddy stream near the railway embankment. As he watches he notices that for a few feet the slab has had the effect of purging the stream of its impure elements, and that the water has even eaten through to a bed of clear pebbles beneath the mud. The man is fascinated by the play of clear pebbles beneath the silt. Despite its superficial resemblance to the 'gleam' that surrounds the bejewelled world of Koomson, 'there seemed to be a purity and a peace here which the gleam could never bring' (p. 23). But as he turns towards the sea he notices that the stream has already started to sully again:

> Far out, toward the mouth of the small stream and the sea, he could see the water already aging into the mud of its beginnings. He drew back his gaze and was satisfied with the clearness of a quiet attraction, not at all like the ambiguous disturbing tumult within awakened by the gleam. (p. 23)

The man's insight here has almost the intensity of a mystical experience. For one blinding moment he is granted an intuition of the moral forces which once ran strong in the mainstream of his people's life. The purity is now corrupted beyond all recognition; ruefully the man is forced to acknowledge the irresistibility of pollution. His intuition in this context has very little relevance beyond itself. Certainly there is no immediate possibility of reform, since the wording implies that the stream is poisoned at its source. Yet against the all-pervading decay the man is able to pit the achievement of his consciousness, however fragmentary and briefly given, of the implicit strength that might, in the longed-for future, enable the stream to clear itself.

A question often asked is whether Armah holds out any hope in the general gloom. The novel's title certainly would seem to suggest a purely temporary set-back. 'The beautyful ones' do not belong to the present time. Even the man and Teacher do not possess the courage and resolution necessary to redeem their own lives, let alone those of others. Their triumph, and it is a limited and flawed one, is that of perspicacity. Like the coals that glow darkly in Milton's Hell, their partial clarity serves to delineate the general morass. When, in Chapter 6, the man berates Teacher for his half-heartedness, Teacher explains his social withdrawal as a reaction to misunderstanding: 'No one wants what I happen to have. It's only words after all' (p. 79). Teacher's statement serves to identify him as a thwarted writer, unable to communicate his message. The implication is far from casual: behind the divisive moral vision of the book lurks the cult of the artist, abused and misunderstood. Perhaps some of the difficulty the reader has in putting his finger on the exact source of the man's awareness is due to the fact that he too shares something of the artist's pertinacity and daring. This may also explain why in his next novel Armah confronts us with a main character whose avowed artistic commitment exposes him to a social ignominy so reminiscent of the man's lone wretchedness.

REFERENCES AND NOTES

1. Ayi Kwei Armah, *The Beautyful Ones Are Not Yet Born* (Boston: Houghton Mifflin, 1968; London: Heinemann Educational Books, 1969). Translated into Swahili as *Wema Hawajazaliwa* (Nairobi: Heinemann (East Africa), 1976). Page references in the text are to the Heinemann Educational Books edition.

2. Eldred Jones, review in *African Literature Today*, vol. 3 (London; Heinemann Educational Books, 1969).

3. Emmanuel Obiechina, review in *Okike* (Nigeria, Nsukka) (April 1971), p. 49.

4. Molly Mahood, 'West African writers in the world of Frantz Fanon', *English Department Workpapers* (Ghana, Cape Coast) vol. 1 (March 1971).

5. Obiechina, *op. cit.*

6. See John Spencer, *The English Language in West Africa* (Harlow: Longman, 1971), p. 3.

7. Margaret Folarin, 'An additional comment on Ayi Kwei Armah's *The Beautyful Ones Are Not Yet Born*', in E. D. Jones (ed.), *African Literature Today*, vol. 5 (London: Heinemann Educational Books, 1971), pp. 116–29.

8. See, for instance, Ronald Hayman, *The Novel Today 1967–75* (Harlow: Longman, 1976), p. 49.

9. Mulk Raj Anand, *Untouchable* (London: Bodley Head, 1970).

10. Ama Atta Aidoo, *No Sweetness Here* (Harlow: Longman, 1970).

3 *Fragments*

▼▼▼▼▼▼▼▼▼▼▼▼▼▼▼▼▼▼▼▼▼▼▼▼▼▼▼▼▼▼▼▼

DESPITE superficial appearances, the title of *Fragments*[1] probably does not refer to its form. Though divided into thirteen sections, each with its own sub-title and perspective on the material, Armah's second novel is probably his most unified, structurally as well as thematically. Its central theme – and the justification for its title – may be found in a statement made by the grandmother in the very last section:

> The larger meaning which lent sense to every small thing and every momentary happening years and years ago has shattered into a thousand and thirty useless pieces. Things have passed which I have never seen whole, only broken and twisted against themselves. (p. 280)

The 'thousand . . . pieces' here are the 'fragments' of the title; the extra thirty pieces are perhaps redolent of the thirty pieces of silver for which Judas Iscariot betrayed Christ. In both cases the sense is one of betrayal and loss.

Naana in her blindness is a seer who is able to perceive ethical realities and truths denied to the rest of society or the other members of her family. This she owes partly to the physical condition which separates her, and partly to her extreme age which supplies her with memories of what things were like before the present rush to material self-improvement. She is as much, if not more, of a visionary than either the man or Teacher in *The Beautyful Ones*, and the spiritual ancestry and rapport she shares with Baako her fragile grandson suggests that she too has the artist's intensity of vision. Significantly her groping, prayerful monologue concerning the way life has been, is, and might be, frames the entire story, lending it direction and emphasis. The language is notably biblical, its tone saturated in the Authorized King James translation of 1611 which has bitten so deeply into the verbal consciousness of the Ghanaian people. Listen, for example, to the closing sentences of the book and compare them to the culminatory dedication of the Revelation of St John the Divine:

> I am here against the last of my veils. Take me. I am ready. You are the end. The beginning. You who have no end. I am coming. (*Fragments*, p. 287)

He which testifieth these things saith, Surely I come quickly. Amen.
Even so, come, Lord Jesus. (Revelation xxii. 20)

In effect Naana's spiritual intuitions may be seen as an almost perfect
fusion of traditional Akan and Christian thought. Seen in the context of
Armah's *œuvre*, they serve to suggest a new direction, for whereas in *The
Beautyful Ones* the organizing focus was sociological and, by implication,
historical, in *Fragments* the deeper concerns centre around a religious
and existential axis.

However, this is to anticipate. The deeper concerns emerge gradually
from the observable details of a story which follows a familiarly tragic
pattern. Baako, the protagonist, a young man of 25, is imminently
expected after a five-year sojourn in the United States, where he has
studied creative writing. From side references we learn that he has, while
in America, already suffered a sort of nervous breakdown, and, in a
flashback, that he has furthermore drastically cut short a proposed
stop-over in Paris, and in an action of hasty almost hysterical flight,
brought forward the date of his arrival in Accra by several days. As a
result, he enters unannounced. His precipitation has been caused not by
gleeful anticipation, however, but by an all-pervasive dread that appears
to follow him everywhere. The act of return has come to bear awesome
implications for him which he cannot control. When asked later by
Juana, his psychiatrist girlfriend, what precisely has caused the disturbance, he eventually answers in a way which neatly delineates one of the
major sources of conflict in the book:

'The worst thing was the fear of the return,' he said.
'What was frightening about it?'
'I didn't know if I'd be able to do anything worthwhile.'
'Has your uncertainty decreased since you came back?'
'I don't know. I don't think so. No.' He was not the flat, hostile
stranger anymore; he was looking directly at her, and she thought she
could see in his eyes an intense desire to have her hear what he was
beginning to tell her.
'Things are getting more definite now,' he began. He talked, very
precisely, of the things worrying him, like a doctor probing into a
diseased body, locating a node of sickened nerves; all his talk was of a
loneliness from which he was finding it impossible to break, of the
society he had come back to and the many ways in which it made him
feel his aloneness. She asked him about his family, thinking of some
possible shelter, but when he spoke of it, his family became only a
closer, intenser, more intimate reflection of the society itself, a concave
mirror, as he called it, and before long she was left in no doubt at all
that in many ways he saw more small possibilities of hope in the larger
society than in the family around him.

'And yet,' he was saying, 'the family is always there, with a solid presence and real demands.'

'Demands that go against those of the larger society?' she asked.

'Well, yes, in a very complicated way,' he said, but instead of going on he made a gesture as if to say that anything else he might say would be useless.

'You don't find working for the family a reasonable hope?' She was trying to trap the idea, to prevent it from escaping.

'It's necessary,' he said. 'I can understand that. But it's changed into something else, something very deeply set now, I think. The member of the family who goes out and comes back home is a sort of charmed man, a miracle worker. He goes, he comes back, and with his return some astounding and sudden change is expected.'

'Is this a new thing, do you think?' she asked him, 'or something with old roots?'

'Now it's taken this modern form. The voyage abroad, everything that follows; it's very much a colonial thing. But the hero idea itself is something very old. It's the myth of the extraordinary man who brings about a complete turnabout in terrible circumstances. We have the old heroes who turned defeat into victory for the whole community. But these days the community has disappeared from the story. Instead, there is the family, and the hero comes and turns its poverty into sudden wealth. And the external enemy isn't the one at whose expense the hero gets his victory; he's supposed to get rich, mainly at the expense of the community.'

'You regret the fact that you studied abroad, then?'

'No,' he said, laughing. 'The same things worry those who stayed here and went to Legon or Kumasi or Cape Coast. Not so fiercely, perhaps, but I've seen some of these fellows. They talk some, and do a lot of drinking. Purposeless, like to keep away things they daren't face. Spend money like some kind of suicide.'

'Does all this leave you confused?'

'It's not confusion. I know what I'm expected to be.' He paused, and she kept herself from interrupting. 'It's not what I want to be.' (pp. 145–7)

There are a number of related problems here, suggesting different angles of approach. Superficially Baako's anxiety is that of any sensitive young man returning to his own country after a prolonged spell abroad: he is worried about whether he can face up to the role now expected of him. But in Baako's case this source of worry is complicated by his exact awareness of those cultural factors which will have moulded his family's probable reaction to him. In his absence, the inarticulate longings of his family will have weaved themselves into a tight web of expectation which threatens him on his arrival. This he very well knows. It is partly to evade the immediate consequences of this that he advances the date of his flight and neglects to send a cable. Avoiding the fanfare of welcome which is his due, he slips in unobserved and spends the first night in an hotel.

Why precisely should Baako be so nervous? Many a returning son in his position has, after a few initial qualms, calmly settled down to the style of life his people have prescribed for him. In the case of Ghana as of many other ex-colonial societies the transition is not always so simple, involving as it does the honouring of certain very strict and definable requirements. The 'been-to' is obliged to provide proof of his residence abroad and earnest of his goodwill towards those to whom he has returned by bearing with him a certain quota of material gifts, luxurious artifacts. If he does not, he is in danger of being considered an outright failure. In such conventional terms, Baako realizes that he is a sadly deficient 'been-to', for he comes bringing neither limousine nor deep-freeze: nothing in fact save a guitar and typewriter and a mere devotion to his lone but ardent craft of writing.

The point of friction between Baako and his people is far from single or simple. It is determined by a whole bunch of attitudes on both sides which shape the areas of conflict. For example, a crude analysis of the attitudes of Baako's family towards him would tend to suggest that they are merely on the make. But a more searching look at the behaviour of Efua, his mother, and Araba, his sister, soon reveals that their preoccupations are neither cynical nor demeaning, feeding as they do off suggestions which emanate from myth. Their love for Baako and longing for his return are undoubted; their absolute assumption that he will bring a car in his wake is one way of paying him homage.

The section in which Baako explains all this to Juana is headed 'Osagyefo', an Akan word denoting a glorious redeemer. Interestingly this was the title which which the Ghanaian people honoured Nkrumah on his emergence, and subsequently one of his official accolades. It tells not only of an endemic potential for hero-worship, but also of a profound longing for release. Baako is the child who has been sent away to forge the weapons of deliverance. His function on his reappearance is hence a sacramental one.

On the plane flying back Baako encounters a certain individual who precisely fulfils the role expected of a successful 'been-to', one Henry Robert Hudson Brempong, B.Sc. In fact this character is clearly something of an old hand at the game, since, as he tells Baako, he has made the journey from Ghana to Europe several times, never empty-handed. The speech with which his sister greets him when he touches down at the airport is both funny and very sad. A travesty of traditional panegyric, it tells us much about the way in which a whole society

has been weaned into regarding its *évolué* children as semi-divine
figures:

> 'Move back, you villagers,' she said, pushing hard against those in her
> way. 'Don't come and kill him with your TB. He has just returned,
> and if you don't know, let me tell you. The air where he has been is
> pure, not like ours. Give him space. Let him breathe!' She pushed till
> she had created some space around the hero. An old woman ventured
> into the space and began to ask a question: 'But how shall we . . .' But
> the fat woman drove her back into the crowd, then whirled around,
> stripping off her large *kente* stole in a movement of unexpected swift-
> ness. She laid the glittering cloth on the asphalt leading to the back
> door of the limousine and called out, 'Come, my been-to; come, my
> brother. Walk on the best. Wipe your feet on it. Yes it's *kente*, and it's
> yours to tread on. Big man, come!'
>   Brempong let her lead him over the rich cloth, nodding and smiling
> as she yelled repeatedly to him, 'Stamp on it, yes, great man, walk!'
> (pp. 84–5)

To this extent then there would seem to be an almost exact correspon-
dence between the demands of the family of the 'been-to' and those of the
wider society beyond. In his conversation with Juana, however, Baako
hints at an underlying source of conflict between these two different
types of obligation. This is significant, since in *The Beautyful Ones Are
Not Yet Born* the family was characteristically seen as but a reflection of
the nation as a whole. In *Fragments*, on the other hand, Baako is seen as
attempting to hold a precarious balance between the two. In order fully to
appreciate this dichotomy we have to consider Baako's position as a
dedicated writer. At the time of his return he has already decided to write
for television rather then to work on novels or poems. He explains his
reasons to Ocran, his old art master at Achimota:

> Ocran gave Baako a tall glass of beer, poured another for himself and
> sat on the floor with his back to the nearest wall and his legs crossed
> easily in front of him. 'So now, Mr. Scribe, what are you going to do?
> Write by yourself?'
>   'I don't think it's possible,' Baako answered. 'I wouldn't want
> to.'
>   'What's so impossible about doing your work alone?'
>   'I don't understand it fully,' Baako said. 'But I've thought a lot
> about it. In fact I went all the way round the bend trying to make up my
> mind.'
>   'It doesn't hurt an artist to taste a bit of madness,' Ocran said. 'But I
> thought a decision to write would be a simple thing.'
>   'Not for me. I had a nervous breakdown over it.'
>   'You didn't want to write, then?' Ocran asked with a small smile.
>   'That's all I've been trained to do. No, that wasn't it, though I felt

like I was cracking up when I first realized it fully. It was like being tricked into a trap. But the real difficulty began after I had accepted that. I couldn't decide what kind of writing I should spend my lifetime on.'

'I see you have the ghost of a missionary inside you, bullying the artist.' Ocran was laughing, but the statement embarrassed Baako. He put his glass to his lips, then looked through the drink and the thick glass bottom and saw a distorted image of the laughing face.

'You can look at it that way,' he said finally. 'Only, I was thinking of it as a way of making my life mean something to me. After all, I had to ask myself who'd be reading the things I wanted to write.'

'You just depress yourself asking those questions,' Ocran said.

'It happened, yes,' Baako said. 'But I came out of it with some sort of a decision. I wouldn't do the usual kind of writing.'

'You decided to give up even that?'

'Not to give up. But if I can write for film instead of wasting my time with the other stuff – it's a much clearer way of saying things to people here.'

Ocran sat staring a long time, as if he had not heard, then he said, 'I know what you're saying. It looks like a hopeless picture, doesn't it? Not too many literate people. And even those who are literate won't read.'

'Film gets to everyone,' Baako said, and he saw the other nod gently. 'In many ways, I've thought the chance of doing film scripts for an illiterate audience would be superior to writing, just as an artistic opportunity. It would be a matter of images, not words. Nothing necessarily foreign in images, not like English words.'

'I understand,' Ocran said. Now he was no longer nodding; he was shaking his head. 'I understand, and what you say is true. But there is something I'd like to tell you. I know you'll think I'm crazy or worse. Anyway, it doesn't matter. If you want to do any real work here, you have to decide quite soon that you'll work alone.' (pp. 113–15)

In the foregoing discussion we can observe a contest between two competing notions of the role of the artist. Ocran, the art master, is heir to the whole post-Romantic European tradition of the artist as a man alone wrestling with a unique destiny. Baako counters this with a vision of the artist very much nearer the traditional African one of a man who serves the spiritual needs of his community. Baako wishes to translate this conception into contemporary terms by using the technologically produced screen image to communicate with the rural masses. It is thus that he hopes to lay his skills at the service of his people and hence fulfil the larger of his two social duties, that to the nation at large.

Paradoxically, it is Ocran's view that proves to be the more socially acceptable. After a frustrating fight with petty officialdom Baako at length lands a job as a scriptwriter on Ghanavision, only to find that nobody in the organization is remotely interested in the lavishly challenging screen plays he proposes. The only form of activity in which his colleagues display the slightest enthusiasm is a slavish following of the movements and pronouncements of the current head of state. A new consignment of television sets, intended for distribution in the rural areas becomes instead the object of frenetic rivalry among the employees of the Broadcasting Corporation itself. Eventually, after a battle of principle with the Head of the Corporation, Baako resigns to commune in separation and silence.

Baako has been attempting to interpret and to practise the traditional role of the artist as best he knows how. It is the very community his attempt was designed to serve which now rejects him. Starved of communication he is forced back onto the perverse, Western notion of the artist as secluded visionary, a pose which possesses at least the elementary dignity of solitude. He uses it to make sense of his own failure and the rejection his people have inflicted on him. His notebooks reveal a search for the source of his country's affliction which he chooses to see in terms of the Melanesian Cargo Cults, an abject awe before material objects which fastens on the returned traveller as intermediary. The comparison has the sort of pertinacity often akin to madness. Indeed there is some sign towards the end of the book that Baako in his isolation is drifting close to a form of schizophrenia he himself acknowledges ('"I am really sick," he said, half in astonishment.' (p. 232)). To his family, however, it is the very fact of writing, rather than the content, which is seen as symptomatic of lunacy. His silence is construed as morbidity, his self-communion as a sure sign of dementia. Discovering him committing thoughts to paper apparently for no eyes but his own, his terrified and bewildered mother sends for his bucolic uncle Foli, who has him committed to a lunatic asylum.

The debate we find here as to the true role of the artist is connected throughout the book with a parallel discussion of religious issues. We have already noted an undercurrent of religious awareness in Armah's work, something which more usually surfaces in his style. Here, however, the issues are open and transparent as when, during their lovemaking, Juana fascinates Baako by adopting a hand posture suggestive of prayer:

'Very Catholic,' he said.
     She laughed. She too had seen the readiness with which her hands made the prayer clasp, but she would have preferred to let her thoughts wander elsewhere. The only time she had asked him, he had told her he had been a kind of pagan all his life, and then he had laughed at her for saying she herself was an atheist. 'You don't act that way,' he had said. 'I think you're a Catholic or, better still, a pagan.' He had offered no explanation, but thinking about the words she had

found an awkward truth about herself. She had had to admit she was concerned with salvation still, though she permitted herself the veil of other names. Too much of her lay outside of herself, that was the trouble. Like some forest woman whose gods were in all the trees and hills and people around her, the meaning of her life remained in her defeated attempts to purify her environment, right down to the final, futile decision to try to salvage discrete individuals in the general carnage. Sometimes she could almost understand the salutary cynicism of Protestants, their ability to kill all empathy, to pull in all wandering bits of self into the one self, trying for an isolated heaven in the shrinking flight inward. She could almost understand it, but even if there were some ultimate peace in it, it would never reach her to change her from within. (pp. 176–7)

At stake in this passage are two contrasting conceptions of a person's spiritual destiny. Firstly, there is the Catholic scheme, which Baako boldly compares to Animism, of a community of spirits saving themselves through pious adherence to a set of recognized rituals: baptism, the mass, and so on. This, suggests Baako, is the braver, more generous course, the one that courts the largest personal risks for a selfless end. Contrasted with this is the Protestant doctrine, which he equivocally calls 'cynical', of personal justification through faith, private integrity of intention brandished as a sort of celestial membership card. The point about Baako, put in these terms, is that he is a convinced Catholic/pagan who is forced through circumstances to take refuge in a timorous Protestant recourse. Attempting to save his people, he trips up drastically and is eventually unable to save even himself. The damnation of lunacy and estrangement follows.

The damnation also of remorse. Like the man in *The Beautyful Ones*, Baako is finally unable to convince himself of the rightfulness of his moral stand. The guilt which results is exacerbated in his case by his fundamental commitment to consulting the interests of others. When he visits Baako in the asylum shortly after his breakdown, the art-master Ocran tries in vain to persuade him of his rightness, the entire propriety of his loyalty to a private artistic vocation. It is Juana, the sensitive psychiatrist, who is able to interpret Baako's resistance to this idea as an expression of divided loyalties between the requirements of his family, who demand material titillation, and the larger community in whose service Baako wishes to sacrifice his own and his family's interests. The conflict is hard to resolve, and Ocran's quasi-Protestant solution of face-saving privacy, the 'shrinking flight inwards' is not one that recommends itself to Baako's temperament. As Juana concludes, talking to Ocran, 'Salvation is such an empty thing when you're alone', a point made even more poignantly by the concluding words of the Nicene Creed which drift

across from the Catholic cathedral over the road towards the end of their
visit to Baako in the asylum:

Et exspecto
resurrectionem mortuorum
et vitam venturi saeculi
Aaaaaaaaaamen. (p. 276)

The novel, then, has two complementary centres of focus: on the one
hand Baako, the struggling individual, and on the other, the society with
which he is desperately trying to relate. The latter focus is trained on a
series of brief, satirical camera shots. The cinematic metaphor seems
appropriate here since Armah's technique is so often reminiscent of that
of the film director. The satirical bite of many of these episodes, however,
brings Armah close to another tradition, that of the pillorying *roman-à-
clef*. Like Kofi Awoonor's novels of Ghanaian life *This Earth My Brother*,[2]
Fragments is an astute portrait of the contradictions involved in a period
of transition, a project which sometimes involves a certain amount of
acrimony. There are several side-glances in it, at personal aggrandise-
ment and public betrayal and, not least, at particular personalities. To
take one instance, Akosua Russell, the sycophantic host of American
influence in the episode set in the Drama Studio, is readily identifiable
with a well-known Ghanaian playwright and poetaster. It has to be said
that in such cases Armah often seems to have sacrificed fairness for the
sake of vividness. The strictures do not always strike true. Nevertheless,
the whole satirical enterprise ultimately justifies itself as an indictment of
the cardinal failings of a people, most pertinently of their creative impotence.

The social weaknesses highlighted in the book correspond exactly with
Baako's own slighted strengths. Baako is misunderstood essentially
because his commitment is to creation, whereas his people are seemingly
incapable of anything beyond a slavish consumption of things which, in
Naana's words, 'we have taken no care nor trouble to produce'. Produc-
tion is to be understood here both in its artistic and material senses, since
the nation's contempt of art is shown as being the logical concomitant of a
wider sterility. Much of the satire serves to accentuate precisely this
point. The painful sycophantism of the producers at Ghanavision, for
example, is a cover for their lack of constructive ideas. The workshop
session at Accra's Drama Studio is diverted from its overt task of
encouraging youthful talent into a fund-raising drive aimed at the
American Ford Foundation. And during Baako and Juana's trek to the
north, a lorry driver, anxious to get his load to market before it rots,
dies in the rush at Yeji ferry. When challenged by Baako, the engineer

in charge of the site is unable to come up with any suggestions as to preventive measures to avoid a recurrence, so dependent is he on the dull treadmill of routine assimilated during an earlier, colonial period.

The notion of sterility here posited is quite fundamental to Armah's social critique in the novel. It is illustrated most poignantly in the outdooring episode which straddles the structure of the book, endorsing its main flow. In effect, this episode and the death of the child which results can be seen as an extended metaphor of the factors which the novelist sees as strangling the nation's instinctual life. Shortly after Baako's arrival, his sister Araba brings forth a child. In Akan custom (for Baako's family would seem to be Ashanti) an uncle's relationship with his maternal nephew is determined in a quite unique way. By tradition, a man, who is spirit, may not bestow to others the properties of the flesh. There is thus no physical relationship between a father and his own child, the physical bond being supplied by the mother. Thus an uncle, who has sprung from the same womb as his sister, the mother, has a stronger kinship with her child than has her own husband. In all matters reflecting on the baby's wellbeing, then, Baako bears a more fundamental responsibility than Kwesi, the father. In the tenderness of his nature, Baako is perfectly prepared to honour these obligations. It is he that rushes the struggling mother to hospital, he that donates the blood to save her life during the delivery. But, when it comes to the outdooring ceremony, he is driven to protest at the way in which Efua his mother and his sister mean to conduct it.

Baako's need to protest springs from his inherited sense of the momentousness of the occasion, something else that he shares with Naana the grandmother. It is she that puts the ceremony in its proper ritual context:

> You know the child is only a traveler between the world of spirits and this one of heavy flesh. His birth can be a good beginning, and he may find his body and this world around it a home where he wants to stay. But for this he must be protected. Or he will run screaming back, fleeing the horrors prepared for him up here. (p. 139)

The ceremony, intended to welcome the child from the world of the ancestors, should be conducted shortly after the eighth day after its birth. But in recent times it has grown into an inflated feast to which the most affluent acquaintances are invited. In this instance Baako's mother proposes to move it back three days from its traditional date to pay-day so as to collect the fattest droppings. At the ceremony itself she expects Baako to stand up splendidly tuxedoed and to call each of the guests in turn to outdo the generosity of the last in a public collection which operates as a kind of monstrous bargaining system. Meanwhile the baby itself is displayed smothered in the folds of an immense *kente* cloth, the effect of which is mitigated by the direct blast of a table fan. To his mother's horror, Baako turns out sensibly clad in a batakari smock and shorts, and limits his speech to a perfunctory announcement. Impatiently she grabs the microphone from him and proceeds to inveigle and embarrass the guests into more and more lavish generosity. Turning aside in disgust, Baako's ear is caught by the tortured cry of the infant. Rushing out to see what is the matter, he discovers that, while its benefactors are falling over one another to demonstrate their affection, the object of their charity has expired in the interval.

The whole outdooring episode is best regarded in the light of an extended metaphor which projects the main concerns of the entire novel. In it we find perfectly blended the two main aims of the book, the double-shaft trained on, first, the public shell of social inanity, and secondly and more pertinently, on the inner spiritual bewilderment. Once again it is Naana who, in a postscript, points the exact significance of what has occurred:

> They have lost all belief in the wisdom of those gone before, but what new power has made them forget that a child too soon exposed is bound to die? What is the fool's name, and what the name of the animal that does not know that? The baby was a sacrifice they killed, to satisfy perhaps a new god they have found much like the one that began the same long destruction of our people when the elders first – may their souls never find forgiveness on this head – split their own seed and raised half against half, part selling part to hard-eyed buyers from beyond the horizon, breaking, buying, selling, gaining, spending . . .
> (p. 284)

Naana's rage here is grounded in an uncanny insight into the collective psychology of her people, an understanding which in turn derives from her perfect attunement with traditional ritual. The death of the child she interprets as a sacrifice made to some weird, modernistic deity. Now in Akan ritual a sacrifice is seen less in terms of placation than of mediation. It is a way of inviting the gods or ancestors to participate in the good things of the clan. The family, she is saying, have wilfully, if unconsciously, done away with their offspring so as to prove their own worth by asserting their equality with those from whom the money offering originally flows: the white men and their local henchmen. Historically this betrayal is connected with the earlier bartering of slaves during the immediate pre-colonial period. It is interesting once again to observe how, in this work as well as in *The Beautyful Ones*, the analysis of present social ills is based on a complete understanding of an entire historical process.

But, if the outdooring episode can be seen in these socio-historical terms, it can also be viewed poetically as an image of sinister, pervasively reverberative force. Infanticide is the ultimate symbol of sterility or impotence. It is as if the perpetrators are deliberately destroying their own capacities to create. A civilization which condones such conduct, even by implication, has to be sick. Deep down one senses that Armah is telling us something of horrendous import, namely that the family have killed the child in resentment at its quick, instinctive life which contrasts so pointedly with their own creative deadness. One would be wary of putting forward such a suggestion if it were not for the fact that it picks up a shock wave that runs through from another of the book's extended poetic metaphors: the killing of the feverous dog in the chapter headed 'Edin'. This is one of the earliest sections and occurs in fact before we have met Baako in the flesh. In effect then, after Naana's opening preamble it stands almost as a preface to the story which follows, and, like the later infanticide image, sends out ripples which converge towards other episodes in the book. Juana, the Puerto Rican psychiatrist, is driving out of town towards Tema after a long, hot day in the surgery. She is just drawing out of Christiansbourg when her progress is halted by a group blocking the road. Gradually she makes out the essentials of the grouping: it consists of several concentric circles of onlookers and, in the centre of attention, a shivering, perhaps rabid dog which is clinging to the tarmac. To one side, ignored by everybody else, is a small boy, owner of the dog, who is pleading for its life. Despite him all the other men are armed for the kill, and it is touch and go who will deliver the decisive blow. Eventually a man with some sort of genital deformity, caused possibly by advanced syphilis, steps forward and dispatches the dog with one brutal blow from his pickaxe. There follows a moment of rapturous climax, tempered however by an instant of embarrassing disquietude, for we read:

> The triumphant killer walked off with his prize in a strange way, as if it were his intention to go through all the motions of a runner while keeping a walker's speed. The drip of life came down from the upturned end of the pickaxe. But from the man himself something else had commenced to drip: down along his right leg flowed a stream of something yellow like a long-thickened urine mixed with streaks of clotted blood. A look of terror stopped the man's triumph as first he felt the drip and then looked down to see what it could be. The fallen child had risen. Seeing the humiliation of the killer of his dog, he was now shouting, laughing through his tears,
>   'Fat balls, hei!'

The boy was still weeping, and the shout had turned his silent grief into a hysterical mixture of suffering for his lost dog and mockery of the killer. But for the killer himself, a wild feeling of relief seemed to have come in place of the first, short fear. Something that had stayed locked up and poisoned the masculinity of his days was now coming down, and in spite of all his shame he seemed seized by an uncontrollable happiness that made him walk with the high, proud, exaggerated steps of a puppet.

'Hei, *tilati*, hei, hei!' the boy shouted again. (pp. 29–30)

Since the man is impotent, unable to impress his sexuality on a woman, he compensates by impressing his brutality on the dog. Frustrated masculinity expressing itself as violence: it is a familiar and entirely comprehensible formula. In the novel it has reverberations way beyond this particular context. One is reminded of the outdooring ceremony, in which a life is sacrificed to exorcize a communal impotence. More crucially still, one recalls the incident towards the end of the book when, just before his incarceration, Baako escapes from the clutches of his family, only to be surrounded by a hectoring, bullying crowd who attempt to trap him with ropes. Here again, the implication is that Baako has been turned into a scapegoat for the weakness of a whole people whose resentment is founded on fear. Indeed if one extends this idea by considering the treatment meted out to Baako throughout the novel, one can see the earlier episode of the dog as a cogent metaphor for the whole work, held in perfect miniature.

One other aspect of Armah's novelistic technique deserves mentioning here. We have already seen that there are occasions on which Armah's episodic method of narration resolves itself in a manner not too dissimilar to a series of camera 'takes'. The flashback, for instance, is a time-honoured ploy of the cinema and one which he deploys throughout this and subsequent works to great effect. It is not only the way in which different phases of the narrative are stitched together, however, that recalls a feature film, but also the way in which many of the individual scenes are realized. The dog episode is a good case in point. The actions described could not possibly have taken more than a few seconds, and yet Armah devotes almost eight pages to their telling, a slowness of rendition that allows him to dwell minutely on such details as the lines traced down the backs of onlookers by runnels of perspiration. The effect of this is to arrest the gestures and movements described to the extent that the reader experiences a sense of suspension not unlike 'slow motion'.

It is not only actions, however, which are described in this way. Often Armah lingers indulgently over passages of pure visual detail in a way which, at first reading, seems a little redundant. Only after some critical attention does the relevance of this technique to the book's human themes become clear. Take, for instance, the description of the passenger lounge at Orly Airport as Baako waits there prior to his departure for Accra:

> Past shiny invitations to a row of elevators and a bar, Baako took a second escalator. A panel at the bottom had promised an art gallery here, but there was only a small maze of bright, empty display boards under the acoustic-tiled ceiling. Beyond the escalators another sign advertised a restaurant open on the floor above:
>
> LES TROIS SOLEILS.
>
> The brilliance of the letters was reflected in the polished floor. Walking round the display boards, Baako found himself listening to the soft sound of falling water, then looking at an indoor waterfall with the water at the bottom illuminated from below. Big hunks of dead wood had been arranged in the water to create an illusion of tropicality. Where the wood stood out of the water it had gone dry, powdery white; but the immersed portions made brown and yellow patterns with the mixture of light and water that made the illusion begin to look alive. Baako placed his typewriter near the pool's edge and bent to touch the water. It was cold, but just behind the biggest log two live ducks were slowly, almost imperceptibly, moving in it as if the cold light from below gave them heat enough. One of them climbed onto the side of the pool, leaving the other alone, and the momentary violence of its motion fractured the shimmering light over the stones at the bottom of the water. Sitting on the containing ledge, Baako watched the two ducks and the logs with the water shaking and falling around and behind them, looking at the ceiling reflected beneath the water when it was nearly still, until a soft pervading female voice from nowhere began repeating in dreamy amplified tones the message: 'Passengers on Air Afrique Flight two-zero-nine Paris, Accra, Brazzaville, please report now at gate number forty-three.' The voice flowed on into German and French with the same studied softness. (pp. 58–9)

What, one might ask, is the purpose of so detailed a descriptive passage at this point in the story? Certainly it slows the pace of narrative advance enough to create an impression of waiting. But do we really need to know the exact number of ducks swimming around the artificial pool, the precise position of the logs, the quality of the light on the surface of the water?

One can finally, I think, say yes: on two different counts. The first is that the description tells us much about Baako's state of mind. You will remember that at this juncture, suspended half-way between New York and Ghana, Baako is in a condition not unlike shell-shock. A disturbance of an unknown but threatening nature has driven him in terror from America, and there has been a recent recurrence in Paris which has sent him scuttling to the airport. Literally and metaphorically, he is in a

process of flight. To a modified extent this is also true of Juana, of whom
we read, just before the dog episode, 'It was not just in the mind, this
need for flight' (p. 17). In effect Baako and Juana are in a similar
situation, driven towards one another by reciprocal needs that neither
entirely understands. The heavy, mesmerized, almost bleary-eyed feel of
both the dog passage and the airport sequence speak of a personal
disorientation only heightened by the intellectual lucidity of those it
afflicts.

The other reason is more complex. The character in *Fragments* exists
in a world where the balance between persons and objects has been upset.
Traditionally in Africa there has always been a considerable reverence for
certain kinds of objects, seen often as the seat of spirits or endowed with
curative or malevolent powers. Yet this reverence was never directed
towards the more physical substance of the object, but rather to certain
mysterious powers held to occupy it.[3] This is in essence the belief
informing animism, a customary way of looking at the world which
Baako compares to Catholicism – viably, since the Catholic notion of
transubstantiation is not dissimilar. Now, however, this deep faith in the
in-dwelling power of essence has been supplanted by an abject awe before
the mere stuff of the object itself. This process can be observed, for
instance, in the libation ceremony performed just before Baako's
embarkation for America. Originally intended, as Naana reveals, as a
compact between the ancestors and the living, it has, like the outdooring
ritual, been transformed into a merely material feast, so that Foli, the
sanguine uncle, scants the invitation to the spirits so as to reserve more of
the precious liquor for his own throat.

Later on in the book, Baako, reminiscing about this episode, comes to
compare it to sacrifices offered in the Melanesian Cargo cults:

> CARGO MENTALITY. The expectancy, the waiting for bounty dropping
> from the sky through benign intercession of dead ancestors, the
> beneficent ghosts. Out there in ancestral territory beyond the cemetery
> the goods are available in abundance, no doubt at all about that in
> Melanesian cargo mythology. Lleweni Ruve: what a beautiful name
> for sheer illusion, though. Wish I had taken notes, or had the books
> somewhere within reach now. The waiting not a simple expectation,
> but something more active. An integral part of the waiting is an active
> expression of strong belief that the cargo will come, i.e., the phenom-
> enon of hope is incomplete without an incorporated act of faith. In
> Melanesia the burning of food crops, the slaughtering of indispensable
> livestock, all those pigs destroyed: an earnest of mortal faith, of the
> belief men have that it is unthinkable the ghosts should fail – if the
> ritual games are played with sufficient seriousness. (p. 228)

Sacrifice a little, the smallest amount possible, of what you already have, and you will reap an impossibly rich reward. Much of the activity observable in the book would seem to shape itself towards this end. The painstaking, almost loving way in which physical objects are described in the text would seem to be a way of suggesting the impassioned ardour and longing with which they are regarded by those who possess them, or, more movingly, the bitter craving of those left outside the charmed circle of owners. This longing is far from narrow or trivial. Corresponding as it does to a displaced mode of worship, it is always described in such a way as to suggest religious intensity. Witness the incident during the distribution of television sets at Ghanavision, when a junior official, prevented from snatching one of the last available appliances by a more fleet-footed colleague, hurls a hunk of concrete in sheer frustrated defiance:

> The strong one laughed a laugh with no regret in it, looking at his fallen companion, then stooped and took the set in his glad embrace, his eyes still on the other. He, the weak one, had the air of one who had given up any notion of continuing the painful contention, but as the strong man hefted the set with his muscular arms and strode confidently forward with it, the fallen man groped and reached a stone sharing the ground with him, and in an unexpected movement hurled it with a hard, desperate force.
> The new set had only a last, brief moment in which to reflect the sunlight in the pearly smoothness of its screen, and then where the brittle glass had been, the hunk of concrete smashed in and left a hole through which it crashed against the copper circuitry within.
> The victor also stood a petrified moment, then dropped the destroyed set, letting out a groan that must have risen all the way from the wreckage of his hot inner desire. He took one quick, desolate look at his shattered dream and then he leaped after his triumphant victim. (p. 217)

The kind of spiritual mutation suggested here is pervasive in the novel. Baako and Juana are its interpreters. Though Juana is not Ghanaian, she exhibits a remarkable empathy with the spiritual tribulations of the country in which she has chosen to work. Driven here by the holocaust of a shattered marriage, she is at first too deeply absorbed in troubles of her own to notice the desolation that lies around her. It is only when she starts to interpret the small signs, the plaintive mottoes on the boards of mammy lorries, the sadness of the highlife song at the Star Hotel, the muted appeal of her patients, that she begins to realize that she is confronted with the symptoms of a malaise which reaches to all levels of society. Like *The Beautyful Ones*, *Fragments* is a book in which the protagonists are gradually brought to an awareness of an underlying sickness. However, whereas in the first novel, the analysis was essentially social and economic, in *Fragments* there is an attempt at a quasi-religious explanation.

There is another major difference between the two books. In *The Beautyful Ones* the strong impression given is that the sickness is a purely Ghanaian affair. The Ghanaian apotheosis of *Fragments*, however, is but the culmination of a prolonged process of withdrawal from the outer edges to the inner core. Starting in America, Baako has escaped, first briefly to France, then back to Ghana, the family and finally the sanctuary of his own mind. At each stage his retrenchment has been accompanied by a recognition of exactly the same cultural symptoms. In Paris, for example, Baako spots a schizophrenic whose disturbance evidently mirrors his own:

> The man gave no sign that he cared or even knew that he was what all these holiday-makers were looking at. He wore no shoes, and he had taken off his shirt, leaving only a pair of faded blue workers' trousers. He had a dark red skullcap on. Suddenly he broke from his immobile stance and marched directly forward as if it was his intention to march straight through the high wall. But a step or two from it he stopped just as abruptly as he had begun, and raised his arms above his head worshipfully, supplicating the wall. He bowed, took seven steps sideways to the right, three to the left, and sat down finally with his legs in something like the lotus position and his head hanging loosely down. On the bridge, Baako felt drawn by an intense interest in what the man down there was doing in his shut-off world, so that without being really aware of what was happening to him he was beginning to try and understand it all, to enter the closed world. (pp. 72–3)

This urge to escape, shut oneself off, is something that Juana has also recognized in her psychoanalytical work. At first she believes it to be due simply to the urban pressures of the capital city, but subsequent journeys in the bush convince her that the disease is spreading everywhere. Indeed when she visits Baako in the asylum just before the end of the book, he reminds her of the name of a town in the countryside which they have both severally visited: it is called 'Bibiani', which means 'This is everywhere'. (pp. 270–1)

The disorientation which Armah is examining in this work then is not something of purely Ghanaian or even African application. Finally it is seen as being nothing less than a salient characteristic of modern civilization. The multiple perspectives displayed in the book are a way of exploring these conditions to the limit of their social and geographical extent. This process is continued and extended in the next novel, *Why Are We So Blest?*

REFERENCES AND NOTES

1. Ayi Kwei Armah, *Fragments* (Boston: Houghton Mifflin, 1970; London: Heinemann Educational Books, 1974; Nairobi: East African Publishing House, 1974). Page references in the text are to the Heinemann Educational Books edition.
2. Kofi Awoonor, *This Earth My Brother* (London: Heinemann Educational Books, 1972).
3. For amplification of relevance to Ghana, see R. S. Rattray, *Religion and Art in Ashanti* (Oxford: Oxford University Press, and the Presbyterian Book Depot, 1959).

4 *Why Are We So Blest?*

▼▼▼▼▼▼▼▼▼▼▼▼▼▼▼▼▼▼▼▼▼▼▼▼▼▼▼▼▼▼▼▼▼

IN contrast with Armah's previous novels, *Why Are We So Blest?*[1] moves from the tight circle of largely Ghanaian concern to embrace a world view, a total vision of the contemporary world whose limits of reference are defined as America, the Muslim Maghreb and sub-Saharan Africa. Its interpreters, who move between these limits in practice or in speculation, are three: Solo, a failed revolutionary who now works as a freelance translator in Algiers; Modin Dofu, a Ghanaian who has recently dropped out of a Harvard degree programme; and his girlfriend, Aimée Reitsch, a white American presumably of German extraction whose ill-defined commitment to the 'revolution' has likewise caused her to abandon her own studies at Radcliffe. The interplay of these personalities is the predominant theme of the book, because *Why Are We So Blest?* marks the point at which Armah has escaped from his earlier intense concentration on the lonely artist figure, trapped by the compulsions and inhibitions of his own ego, and moved towards the problem of evolving a notion of communal redemption. Various versions of possible salvation are proffered in the book; none is finally compelling. There is some sign also, in at least two of the central figures, of a retention of the suffering protagonist, and the novel closes on an elegiac note of loneliness.

Structurally the book is more complex than even *Fragments*. Not only does it leap forward and backwards in time, sometimes with seeming perversity, but it also employs three narrators, as well as the central authorial voice. Each of the three main characters is given a chance to explain their predicament unedited, into camera as it were. For much of the text Armah resigns his narrative and explicative function to Solo, with whose weary view of things the authorial consciousness ultimately merges. Solo's narrative, however, is interleaved with snatches from the diaries of both Dofu and Aimée. It is only comparatively late in the novel that we learn the reason for this: after Modin's death Aimée has entrusted the notebooks to Solo for safe keeping. Solo's reminiscences, however, can be assumed to have been compiled after he gets his hands on the diaries, so that, in commenting on the other two personalities, he has the benefit of their own self-revelation as well as his own observation. It is perhaps one of the more frustrating aspects of the work that the same process does not work in reverse: neither Modin nor Aimée seem to consider it worth their while discussing Solo, considering this 'failure' perhaps to be beneath their contempt. In the case of Aimée one cannot be said to feel the loss: there is precious little love lost between her and Solo, and, despite some initial attraction on his part, their cumulative relationship is one of mutual loathing. In the case of Modin, the comments would be worth having. There is a considerable empathy between these two tortured beings, and some similarity of temperament. The empathy, however, is largely evidenced by Solo's sympathetic reading of Dofu's diaries, at a time when he is already helpless to intervene. In reminiscences, however, he establishes a considerable imaginative rapport with his Ghanaian acquaintance. It is one of the finest paradoxes of this work that the most worthwhile relationship in the book is, as to some extent in *Fragments*, that which is never given conversational expression. In *Fragments* the core of the work was the rapport between Baako and his grandmother. In this work it is that between Solo and the slightly younger Dofu, a classic case of unrequited love.

The characters meet in a North African capital called Laccryville, which is quite obviously meant to be taken for Algiers. What has driven these three lost souls, two black Africans and one white American, to this spot on the Mediterranean littoral? The question is important, because it provides the frame for their individual quests, each seeking in the capital city of independent Algeria something that elsewhere they have lost sight of. For Solo, Algeria is frankly a refuge. A native of one of the enslaved Portuguese territories, called for convenience here 'Congheria', he has spent some time in the Maquis engaged in his country's cause, only to be driven back by an undefined failure. Whether his failure was one of nerve or of commitment is not explained. In either case it has left him with a vast overload of guilt, and a general sense of himself as an ideological neuter, one of the world's supernumeraries.

> We are easy to recognize. Our personalities are battlefields on which our subjective demands meet the harsher demands of life and time. While the battle goes on we are crippled by inactivity and depression. And the battle goes on seemingly forever. I know. I, who have so little confidence left that I spend my time asking myself whether it is not only the arrogant fool who would want to offer truthful statements to people who must live. It is this lack of confidence which deepens into the despair of the guilty whenever I go out without first taking care to hide myself from the truths outside. (pp. 14–15)

Solo wastes his time in trivial pursuits and the occasional burst of translating, and in hanging around the offices of the People's Union of

Congheria, seat of the government in exile, where he seems to have the status of an affectionately regarded invalid, to be tolerated but not trusted.

The offices of the People's Union of Congheria, too, are the initial destination of Modin and Aimée, who have both hitched across Europe from America. Their choice is not random. We can assume that the date of action is approximately 1965, at which period Algeria, having only recently wrestled a mean independence from the French yoke, had become the stamping ground of revolutionaries of all shades of persuasion, and a home from home for struggling nationalist movements. In deciding to come here then, Modin and Aimée are obeying partly modish considerations. In a word, Algeria is fashionable, if you happen to be a self-styled revolutionary. For Aimée, one senses that that is the sum of it. Impelled by the sort of awkward destructive restlessness that is for ever seeking new pastures to lay waste, she impresses herself irresistibly as a creature of mere impulse. In deciding to come to Algeria she is obeying the same kinds of consideration that may have driven her to wear jeans, or to stop eating popcorn. One senses, as does Solo, the superficiality of her position throughout: she is responsible for some of the most gauche, most laughably naïve comments in the book. Modin, however, is a creation of a different water. He has opted out of Harvard, where he was studying on an American scholarship, not from Aimée's kind of restlessness, but from a deeply considered mistrust of an educational process that would seem to be aimed at alienating him from his people. His decision to come to Algeria and offer his services to the Congherian cause is an attempt to give physical expression to his dissent, and to justify his privileges through some concerted course of action:

> Leaving with no positive direction would be a static act, a mere show of refusal, a gesture. Stupid, dishonest. No use getting out if I can't work out a positive direction to go in. Yet at the moment I find a positive direction impossible to choose. All my past training has oriented me in negative directions. The positive direction is the maquis. I have no skills for going that way. (p. 223)

Modin's tragedy is twofold. First, he is saddled with Aimée, from whose ravenous clutches he is loath to extract himself, and who has the further effect of diluting the sincerity of his purpose to the extent where it is unacceptable to the Congherian authorities. Secondly, his élite course of liberal education has left him ill equipped to engage in a proletarian struggle. His crisis of conscience is of no interest to those who control entry to the Maquis: they want practical skills.

The Algeria towards which these distracted exiles have gravitated is not a country which would seem to lend any support to their highest deals. It is independent, but poverty, degradation, mutilation are observable everywhere. The sense one has is that this desolation is due, not simply to the inevitable dislocation of a recent war, but rather to a sell-out by the new national government which is so anxious to court French and international favour that it has neglected the more pressing task of revitalizing the economy. Towards the beginning of the book Solo's perpetual remorse has driven him to a state of mental breakdown. Admitted into hospital he encounters in the library a *mutilé de guerre*, who is reading his way through the histories of various revolutions in search of an answer to the question 'Who gained?' Is abandonment by the newly established government of those who brought them to power inevitable? *L'essence de la révolution, c'est les militants*,' he says, so why are they left to feed off the droppings of the new cadre of rulers? Solo's eventual answer comes in the form of a drawing, in which he exploits the two available senses of the French word *'l'essence'*: *'l'essence*, that which is essential; and *l'essence*, petrol' (p. 26). His drawing is of a lorry:

'You are right', I said. 'The militants are the essence. But you know, that also means they are the fuel for the revolution. And the nature of fuel ... you know, something pure, light, even spiritual, which consumes itself to push forward something heavier, far more gross than itself.'

For some moments he was quiet, as if he was having to think of what I had just said. Then he spoke, quietly.

'What is it you wrote in the notebook?'

'Just what I said.'

He took the notebook and looked at it.

'And the drawing?' he asked.

'The truck represents society. Any society. Heavy. With the corrupt ones, the opportunists, the drugged, the old, the young, everybody, in it. And then there are the militants, pushing the whole massive thing from the lower to the higher level. But they themselves are destroyed in the process.'

'That is what you believe?' he asked.

'That is what seems to happen,' I answered. 'You yourself were saying it.'

He looked at the drawing. Underneath its calm surface, his face was the face of a man who wanted to fight against a horrible truth but could not find any way to do it. Finally, he asked a question to which I knew he expected no answer.

'*Mais c'est juste? C'est juste?*'

All the same I shook my head in impotent sympathy.

'No,' I said. 'It is not just. Not at all.' (p. 27)

Once again, Armah would seem to be probing beneath the surface of corruption, to detect via Solo something of the underlying cause. Solo's agnosis leads towards a complete analysis of social motivation, a

causality that transcends the particulars of the given case. Algeria's fate i
that of every Third World country groaning under a cumbersom
administration. The model is clear: social success lies via alienation fron
and abandonment of the masses. It is the logical result of a colonia
process of education. Aggravated in Francophone countries such a
Algeria by the direct assimilation policy, it nevertheless correspond
fairly exactly with the system of promotion and advancement in al
segments of the erstwhile imperial world. Solo, from a Portuguese col
ony, has felt it intimately, but the most cogent description of it come
elsewhere. An extract from Modin's journal reads:

> Knowledge about the world we live in is the property of the alien
> because the alien has conquered us. The thirst for knowledge therefor
> becomes perverted into the desire for getting close to the alien, getting
> out of the self. Result: loneliness as a way of life.
>
> This loneliness is an inevitable part of the assimilationist African'
> life within the imperial structure. Because of the way information i
> distributed in the total structure – high information in the center, low
> information on the peripheries – overall clarity is potentially possibl
> only from the central heights. The structures in the peripheral area
> are meant to dispense low, negative or mystificatory information.
>
> The choices are clear. Those who stay in the peripheral areas intel
> lectually, emotionally, psychologically, totally, are not lonely. The
> are in touch with home, not cut off. The price they pay for not bein
> lonely, however, is that they suffer the crudest forms of manipulation
> mystification, planned ignorance.
>
> Those who shift from the periphery to the center can hope to escap
> some of these cruder forms of manipulation. But the price they pay i
> loneliness, separation from home, the constant necessity to adjust t
> what is alien, eccentric to the self. All this is in the present structurin
> of the machinery for acquiring knowledge, not in the essential natur
> of the learning process itself. (pp. 32–3)

Modin himself has experienced the whole 'learning process' in what h
regards as a particularly virulent form during his years in America
Indeed the whole American sequence of the work, which is glimpsed i
flashback extensively through extracts from Dofu's journals, and frag
mentarily through Aimée's, can be read as a kind of prolonged disserta
tion on precisely this 'learning process'. To some the American episode
will seem the least satisfactory in the book. Indeed certain passages ar
only tolerable when seen in the light of a meditation, cast in bold relief
upon this very theme of alienation. The satire is cutting, cruel, and one i
sometimes left, as in *Fragments*, with the feeling that it has overshot it
mark. The justification can only lie in the clarification of certain struc
tured concerns, among which educational 'assimilation' is prominent

From the moment of his arrival in the States, Modin's clear-sighted intelligence perceives the implications of his training with great insight; perceives, for instance, that he has been taken into the fold from the very first on sufferance. From the beginning he is made to feel that the clue to his acceptance lies not in the fact that he is able – that in the Ivy League atmosphere of Harvard presumably is commonplace enough – but that he is an intelligent *African*, something hardly to be thought of. Take for instance the welcoming remarks of Mr Oppenhardt, Chairman of the Committee of the foundation which is funding Modin's scholarship:

Mr. Oppenhardt was first: 'All your confidential reports say you are a most unusually intelligent African – the most intelligent as a matter of fact.'

'That is not true, sir,' I said.

'There's no need to get modest about a thing like that. You obviously are.'

'Boakye and Kantara . . .' I did not know exactly what I was going to say. I was confused. Many names filled my head, the names of all my friends these people would never know. It was stupid to judge my intelligence against them all, but how could I let these people know when they did not want to listen?

'Let me finish, boy,' said Mr. Oppenhardt. I was surprised by the voice. The other men looked worried, the professor most of all. His mouth was tight. Looking at him, it occurred to me he was trying to show me the best thing to do in the situation. I shut my mouth.

'It's because of your unusual intelligence that you're here,' Mr. Oppenhardt continued. There was silence, and he looked happier. 'Don't ever apologize for that. You have earned everything you've got. I hope you'll continue to earn even more, by recognizing the special intelligence that has set you apart, and never hesitating to use it.' (p. 120)

Despite Modin's continuing protests, the Committee persist in regarding him as some kind of performing animal. It is in vain that he counters by mentioning friends back home every bit as gifted as he. For Oppenhardt and his kind Modin's intelligence is 'unusual', not because he has proved himself smarter than his classmates, but because they regard intelligence as a Caucasian reserve, and hence must applaud the efforts of anybody who has been able to force himself through the palings. There is a certain danger implicit in this acceptance though; Modin must never be regarded as a herald of the great African host. If he is, then the palings will be trampled underneath in the rush to enter. Rather must he be persistently marked out as an exceptional case, proving by his very existence the general rule of African idiocy. It is to this underlying assumption that Modin reacts. And if his reaction lacks grace, then his reasons are cogent. He rejects a scholarship offered on these humiliating terms, for to accept the money would be to accept the assumption underlying it. His hosts are suitably outraged.

Racial insult, however, is not the worst that Modin has to fear. He has next to endure an indoctrination process, all the more insidious for being largely implicit in the objective training he is given. Modin is only safe in so far as he can be taken as exceptional: no efforts then are spared to see to it that he is made aware of the growing gap between him and his countrymen, and, where possible, to widen that gap. The student, regarded as a potential leader, must be made into the perfect factor or go-between between his own race and the Europeans, who in this manner continue to wield ultimate power. In a late passage Modin compares the lot of these *évolués* to the 'factors' or slave-minders who in earlier centuries exercised control over their own people in the name of the white slave-trader (this is a very similar analogy to that used about Koomson in *The Beautyful Ones*):

> Factors then, scholarship holders, B.A.s, M.A.s, Ph.D.s now, the privileged servants of white empire, factors then, factors now. The physical walls stand unused now. The curious can go and look at them as if slavery belonged to a past history. The destruction has reached higher, that is all. The factor's pay is now given in advance, and sold men are not mentioned, not seen in any mind. Their price is given the factor for some mythical quality of his dead spirit. His murdered intelligence is praised. The easier for the givers of these scholarships, this factors' pay, to *structure* the recipients' lives into modern factorship. (p. 161)

One result of this is the sickening knowledge of betrayal that all who receive such training must carry with them. Another and more immediately stinging result is a sense of isolation which is twofold: isolation from white mentors or peers who have nothing but contempt for the background from which the student has emerged, and, more cruelly, isolation from one's own people. The latter in the first place consists in mere physical isolation, a circumstance which Modin himself alleviates soon after his arrival by taking up with Oppenhardt's black secretary, Naita. As time wears on, however, the subtler sort of estrangement becomes apparent, that of attitude and aspiration, and the professional direction in which the student's studies inevitably lead him.

Throughout his American experience, then, Modin is tortured by a feeling of very real loneliness. There are various ways of alleviating this, but all appear on inspection to be traps. The first and easiest is that of flattering the expectations of eager hosts, a sheer obsequiousness of which Modin is temperamentally incapable. The second, and more attractive, is by exploiting the perennial Western taste for the exotic. Deep down in the heart of every white woman, it appears, there is a irresistable urge to be sexually assaulted by some virile primitive (who will be, by definition, black). There are certain very obvious advantages to fulfilling this need, and Modin for one is not blind to the charms of Mrs Jefferson, wife of an aging Africanist who has taken a condescending interest in his welfare. The affair regresses through coitus to mutual masturbation and would presumably have reached even more fascinating depths had it not been for the interference of the enraged professor who, surprising them in the course of their lovemaking, dispatches Modin to hospital with multiple dagger wounds. For some young men this peccadillo would have flattered a sense of personal worth. Modin, however, is much too perceptive to be under any illusions on that score: he was, he knows, merely catered for Mrs Jefferson's endemic craving for something wild, exciting and out of the ordinary. Accepted academically despite being black, he is laid sexually *because* he is black. While the latter might seem superficially preferable, both methods of approach are in effect ways of denying his common humanity, the individuality that makes him a distinct person. Disillusionment hardens into a deep distrust, and Modin is back where he started, alone.

Having avoided the temptations of sycophancy and sexual dishonesty, Dofu then falls for the last and most deadly of pitfalls: pity. Deprived of his scholarship, and hampered by the wounds inflicted on him by the professor, he has recourse to the university's applied psychology laboratories, where he earns a pittance as a guinea-pig for practical experiments. One experiment is of particular interest: shocks are delivered through wires connected to the subjects' ankles in order to test the threshold of pain. Modin cries out when the dial has reached a perfectly average 5·1, but one of the subjects tested has a threshold of pain which extends beyond the prescribed safety levels: one Aimée Reitsch. It is Modin's first encounter with the girl who will dog him for the rest of his life. Like the others, Aimée pursues Modin for possible sexual excitement. Modin's response is in this case motivated not by deceit or idle lust, but gentler considerations. Aimée is frigid, and Modin mistakenly takes it upon himself to awaken her to the full range of sexual experience, not realizing that for her more than curiosity is involved. Not before it is too late, Modin discovers that he is entwined in a complex emotional way barely distinguishable from love.

From the outset it is necessary to admit that there is a certain problem connected with the portrayal of Aimée in the novel. Her character is indubitably central, vital indeed in that of all the characters hers is the most instrumental in bringing about the final catastrophe. The trouble is that she appears simply in this light, as the agent of destruction. The description given of her by Solo, whose words carry immense weight

throughout, is actively hostile. Despite his evident affection for her
Modin too is noticeably cautious. Such extracts as are given from her own
journals serve merely to incriminate her. If her personality is to be
construed in a purely naturalistic sense, the reader's sense of equity is
likely to be outraged. The only way round this problem is to take her, not
as an individual person, but as a matrix for all those vices which Modin
comes to see as most characteristic of white America. Viewed thus, she
becomes a crucial element in Modin's progressive disenchantment, a way
through to the heart of the American, hence the European, trauma.

Her sexual frigidity, for instance, is of this order. It is consistently
portrayed as but an aspect of wider lack of responsiveness, of which her
monstrous toleration for pain is another. Whether these two very
different kinds of insensitivity normally co-exist is questionable, but
hardly, in the context, germane. The fact is that Aimée's responses, like
those of most of her compatriots, have been dulled to any but the most
extreme stimuli. Hence the massive injection of pain needed for her to
register discomfort. Hence her inability to react erotically in the first
instance to Modin's advances. Hence the lavish, and somewhat risible
phantasies in which she must indulge before experiencing even the
slightest sexual tremor. Symbolically these are all of a kind, consisting in
a banishing of natural instinctive life to the outer limits of sensation. It is
as if the mind has divorced itself from the nervous system and taken off
into some bizarre Walt Disney orbit of its own. Poverty of the emotional
as much as of the mental life is the result.

Her symptoms in this respect are shared by all of the other white
characters. Mrs Jefferson, for example, has recourse to Modin's atten-
tions because she has ceased to be aroused by matrimonial relations with
her husband. It is suggested at one point that Professor Jefferson is
impotent, or at least sexually diffident. The same scourge would seem to
afflict the Oppenhardts' marriage. The symptoms are tragic: the worst
that one can say for Modin's, and by implication Armah's, account is that
it lacks the faintest tincture of that compassion which usually accompanies recognition of tragic facts. The disturbance, however, is not seen
simply as an organic racial incapacity. The sexual clumsiness is shared
evidently by those members of the African élite who have been subjected
to the process of alienation already discussed. Some months prior to her
meeting with Dofu, Aimée has devoted one academic year to teaching
and research in an East African country which strongly resembles
Kenya. While there she has a couple of sexual encounters with former
leaders of the Moya Moya (Mau Mau?) rising, now big shots in the
nationalist government. In both instances, according to her own logged
account, the experience was one of sexual frustration and disappoint-

ent. The account here reflects as much on the boorish incompetence of
ne males as it does on Aimée's admitted inhibitions: they simply did not
are. The episode is significant in that it demonstrates once again the
nstinctual sacrifice that is inevitably involved in adoption into the neo-
olonialist structure. Once again the logic, circumstantially suspect,
arries considerable symbolic weight.

The remainder of the American sequence is devoted to the instinctual
beration of Aimée, won at every stage at Modin's expense. He takes
pon himself the somewhat cumbersome role of sexual tutor, little
nowing how much of himself he is giving away with each bout of
nstruction. Much of the effect of these developments will be lost,
owever, if we come to see Dofu here as purely and simply the unwitting
ctim of Aimée's exploitation. At every step his compliance is an evident
art of the process, since it must be seen that the course of instruction,
ne obverse of Modin's lamented 'learning process', is achieved on
odin's own terms. If Modin had been content to be used sexually as he
as by Mrs Jefferson, nothing but disappointment and humiliation
ould have ensued. Indeed, this is precisely how Aimée attempts to
nploy him, as an object to stimulate her phantasy life, with which her
xual life is initially identical. It is Modin who refuses this role, and
nce forces through a passage to a deeper personal relationship. At one
oint Aimée is close to achieving an orgasm when she is brought to a
pid stop by Dofu who realizes that she has, in phantasy, been indulging
the embraces not of himself, but of a pet creature of her dream life, a
ack servant figure called Mwangi. On these sick terms, Modin is
willing to complete the coupling. Aimée must learn to relate to him in
s full individual humanity before intercourse will have any meaning.
his recoil from the vicarious sexual compensation of Mrs Jefferson and
r kind, however, only leads Modin into trouble, since it involves him in
calamitous personal relationship with the rapacious Aimée. By the time
r sexual education is completed, the tutor is well and truly embroiled,
nce we read in a brief journal entry:

The disgust I began to feel with Aimée is gone. A tenderness I cannot
explain has replaced it. (p. 213)

odin has won. He has lead Aimée into a state of significant love, only to
ll into a, for him, disastrous reciprocation.

Throughout these American passages there is much talk of death.
deed at times Modin seems to view his induction into the American
ay of life as but a mode of dying. There are many reasons for this which
mediately recommend themselves, but we should beware of interpret-
g these remarks in the light of the archetypal equation between sex and

death which is so prevalent in European culture. It is true that, in
merging himself with Aimée, Modin is to a certain degree dying unto
himself, but not in the sense suggested by the Elizabethan use of the word
'die' familiar to us, for example, from Shakespeare's sonnets. Modin's
threatened death is of a much more concrete kind. It is he who has the
earliest premonition of it:

> The pain is terrible. The more I think of what has happened, the
> harder I find it to escape the same conclusion: I am fated to undergo
> some form of death. There is no sanctuary. I have known periods of
> spiritual death when I have shut myself up away from this world.
> There is loneliness that is a kind of death. But the solution available,
> involvement with these people, is itself a deeper form of death.
>
> I find it bad that I should have to run away from knowledge of the
> deeper wounds, the spiritual damage awaiting me in these involve-
> ments, till a physical wound forced on me the necessity to think of
> what my life here has been about. This escape from knowledge of
> myself is unhealthy. (p. 159)

The passage occurs immediately after the assault by Professor Jefferson.
Clearly Modin sees the threat of physical death as but an extension of the
slow paralysis of the soul he earlier calls loneliness. And the sort of
loneliness he experiences in America is indeed that, since it involves a
denial of a very important part of himself. Yet the escape route runs
straight into the cul-de-sac of yet another kind of death, the denial of
cultural identity. From this point on Modin makes every effort to
attempt to meet Aimée on common ground, even to the extent of dressing
like her. The falsity of this is immediately sensed by the intuitive Solo as
soon as he sees the pair together in the Congherian offices in Laccryville:

> At first sight I had noticed the contrast they made – one black, the
> other white. What struck me now, as I went closer, was how similar
> they had tried to make themselves. I looked harder. It was true.
>
> From top to bottom the two wore identical clothes: coarse-woven
> blue shirts in the American style with their collars held down by small
> buttons, light-colored cowboy jeans with nothing to hold them up,
> thick white socks and very strong canvas shoes with thick soles and a
> blue line over each toecap. Two people, so different, yet so willfully
> assimilated. The thought came to me: here was an acute case of love.
> Or ... A smile threatened to force itself to the surface. I was able to
> suppress it. Their clothes were not the only identical things they had.
> There were also burdens on their backs: soldiers' camping knapsacks
> made from green cloth over an aluminium frame. (p. 56)

Elsewhere Solo notes Modin's small 'cat-like' movements which contrast so incongruously with his outward-bound style of dress. The
compromise then has been Modin's: he has accommodated himself to

Aimée's taste and physical personality. It is the beginning of the last and most drastic kind of death, the complete surrender of his own identity, the conscious laying of himself on the altar of Aimée's emotional rehabilitation. Aimée does not spare to take up the knife.

The upshot is soon told. Modin and Aimée apply formally to enter the Maquis, but their statements are torn up in their absence and they are fobbed off by excuses and delays. They hang around the town's cheaper pensions in a state of restless suspense: they have deliberately chosen the meanest hotels since, as Solo remarks, Aimée in her adolescent way seems to equate revolution and dirt. When their funds are exhausted, they come and stay briefly with Solo, who is thus able to witness the hysteria which is driving Modin towards ruin. Eventually in sheer desperation they decide to trek across the desert on their own initiative. Despite Modin's realistic reluctance, Aimée urges him on because 'What would I look like telling people I didn't cross the Sahara after all' (p. 283). After a period of mounting tension between the lovers, they are picked up by a crew of marauding OAS terrorists, who castrate Modin and leave him dying. Aimée is raped and released, after which she returns illogically to reproach Solo with what has happened. Solo, despite her threats, retains possession of the notebooks which act as a source for his narrative.

The harshness of this close is tempered by a note of elegy, for it is with touching sincerity that Solo acknowledges his grief:

> A sense of loss came over me. Modin had never listened to me, never heard me. That did not matter. Over my mind he exercised an influence of whose exact nature I am still ignorant. I wept for him, in impotent acknowledgement of a destiny shutting both him and me within its destructive limits. (p. 271)

Here, it seems to me, we are at the glowing centre of the book. Solo's obituary tribute is occasioned partly by the recent news of Modin's death, and partly by the overwhelmingly poignant message that has come across to him after reading through the latter's notebooks, speaking of a loneliness and despair he only too sadly recognizes, and confirming the unspoken rapport he has felt for the doomed Ghanaian ever since his first appearance. Solo has from the very first diagnosed Modin's condition, yet, inhibited by Aimée's presence, and his own sense of unworthiness, has been powerless to warn. Again and again he returns to this theme:

> I found no way to help him. Help: the word is conceited, coming from me. Between us the distance was so great. I spoke words to him, but sounds from the world I had re-entered did not reach him.
>
> Where he hoped to go I had already been. I had run back with a spirit broken by too sudden contact with real arrangements, my mind howling for peace, any mediocre peace. What help had I to offer him?

To what would I have called him? Had he listened to my warnings, been drawn back by my voice calling him across the distances between, what would I have given him? For his mind, no refuge. The saving hand prepares resting places for bodies exhausted elsewhere. The saving mind creates spaces for the soul in flight, spaces giving rest. What he needed I could not create. (p. 83)

And again:

What would I have called him to? He saw my life. Everything I am, everything I do was transparent to him. Between us he kept that endless distance, an insulating vacuum giving him clear sight, making nonsense of anything I could have said to him. (p. 137)

Finally then we are back with Solo's withered consciousness, his all-involving sense of failure. In this, and the crucifying guilt that accompanies it, Solo is not unlike Baako, not unlike 'the man'. He is like them too in his artistic awareness: like Baako, he sees himself as a failed writer, caught between two schools of art:

Why not simply accept the fate of an artist, and like a Western seer, close my eyes to everything around, find relief in discrete beauty, and make its elaboration my vocation? Impossible. The Western artist is blest with that atrophy of vision that can see beauty in deliberately broken-off pieces of a world sickened with oppression's ugliness. I hear the call of that art too. But in the world of my people that most important first act of creation, that rearrangement without which all attempts at creation are doomed to falseness, remains to be done. Europe hurled itself against us – not for creation, but to destroy us, to use us for creating itself. America, a growth out of Europe, now deepens that destruction. In this wreckage there is no creative art outside the destruction of the destroyers. In my people's world, revolution would be the only art, revolutionaries the only creators. All else is part of Africa's destruction. (p. 231)

Thus speaks Solo the translator, with one half of his mind. But there is another half too, hesitant, questioning: the temperament that needs these culminating absolutes to paste over its own deep uncertainty. In a foregoing paragraph, Solo has written, 'What would I not give to attain the healing simplicity of hatreds unmixed with love?' It is this perhaps that attracts him to Modin, a personality in some ways at fundamental variance with his own: the willingness to make absolute, uncompromised assertions without fear of the reasonable qualifications that might undermine their decisiveness. Solo himself is too conscious of the good things about Europe/America, their art, their written and transmitted culture, to take this sort of a stand. He is too intimately stirred by the 'discrete beauty' a rapprochement with Europe offers to him. Without this kind of background, with only his unequivocal and humiliating experience to guide him, Modin is able to play the affirmative and polemic role, while Solo hangs around in the wings hankering after an impossible beauty.

The only solution for Solo, as suggested in the above passage, is to lay his art at the service of his people. This was Baako's aim in *Fragments*, a modern version of traditional communalist art. It is the equivalent, too, of Modin the student's project of putting education and training at the disposal of the revolution. Indeed, it is Modin who offers the shrewdest analysis of such a programme of action. In one of the earlier American sequences Modin is taken to task over his socialist principles by Mike, a Republic minded fellow student who reads out to him a complacent self-congratulatory editorial out of one of the Sunday newspapers, the title of which, 'Why are we so blest?', gives the novel its title. The article proposes a rather literate version of the American Dream, according to which the New World is the paradisal top storey of a three-tier universe, a model derived from the Greeks. The bottom storey in this arrangement represents the 'communal dirt', while in the space in between blunder those who, by dint of special ability or effort, are granted the privilege accorded to 'cross-overs', those whose honorary membership of the celestial club provides evidence of a special grace, and hence justifies an otherwise unbearably hierarchical system. Mike's placing of Modin in this cosmos is of interest, as is Modin's considered repost:

'Modin, you're nobody's plaything. That's vulgar. The question is deeper than that. You're a scholarship student. There's justice in that. You belong here. The arrangement that brings you here has to be a good arrangement. In the Greek tradition you'd be a cross-over. One of those who rise from the plains to live on Olympus. A hero. Part man, part god. Therefore more interesting than either.'
'Even staying in your mythology, you shut out the Promethean factor.'
'I guess that's a reverse crossover. No. I didn't want to shut it out. But it's unique. Besides, who has the idiotic ambition to go through the crossing twice: first a heroic, than a Promethean crossing? That's insane.'
'Only according to your mythology. There are other myths, you know.' (pp. 101–2)

The classical references here may need some explanation. Prometheus was one of the earliest deities, the Titans. Having created man out of clay, he wished to convey to him the gift of fire, but was opposed in this by Zeus. Despite this he stole fire from Olympus and took it down to men, whereupon Zeus chained him on Mount Caucasus, where his entrails were continually fed upon by a vulture. The analogy is with Modin's proposed course of action. After receiving higher training in America he wishes to return to Africa to put it at the disposal of the masses. In this he will be opposed by Oppenhardt and his kind who will wish him to reserve a certain amount of knowledge to himself so as to make himself a more efficacious neo-colonial agent. If despite this he persists, he will be forced to suffer a lingering agony, in this case the pangs of loneliness and alienation.

Both Solo and Modin fail in this, as did Baako and the man before them. Nevertheless, the Promethean model stands as the most helpful and potentially useful notion of the artist's role to emerge from these books. It is proposed in one form or another in each of them, deploying a different myth each time. In *The Beautyful Ones*, it is the myth of the cave from Plato; in *Fragments* the local myth of Osagyefo; here it is Prometheus. Despite this, none of these works can be said to put the project into effect. To do so would involve a fundamental realignment of the novel, the abandonment of the bewildered artist-protagonist, and the adoption of a communal, plural voice. This is precisely the plan of campaign adopted in Armah's fourth novel, *Two Thousand Seasons*.

REFERENCE AND NOTE

1. Ayi Kwei Armah, *Why Are We So Blest?* (New York: Doubleday, 1972; London: Heinemann Educational Books, 1974; Nairobi: East African Publishing House, 1974). Page references in the text are to the Heinemann Educational Books edition.

5 Two Thousand Seasons

▼▼▼▼▼▼▼▼▼▼▼▼▼▼▼▼▼▼▼▼▼▼▼▼▼▼▼▼▼▼

THE reader who turns straight from *Why Are We So Blest?* to the opening pages of *Two Thousand Seasons*,[1] Armah's fourth novel, is immediately struck by a crucial difference. Where before there was a clear narrative structure which, though flexible and involved, moved between fixed and definable points, here we are treated to a fictional panorama which apparently recedes into the far distance. Where before we enjoyed a highly distinctive evocation of a particular historical period, normally the late 1960s, here we are confronted with immense and almost immeasurable tracts of time. Where before our attention was arrested by specific and intriguing personalities, here we are obliged to make our way through many pages before happening on a use of the third person singular, let alone a proper name. Most importantly, where before we searched in vain for an instance of recognizable authorial intervention, here we find the writer taking upon himself a role of obtrusive commentator from the very first sentence.

Those familiar with the three earlier novels are likely to be, not merely surprised, but also alarmed. While there was plenty in those previous works to challenge one's social and cultural complacency, there is nothing in their technique to disorientate someone versed in the development of twentieth-century fiction. *Fragments*, for instance, is technically a work of immense resource; yet the devices on which the author draws in both this and *Why Are We So Blest?* – flashbacks, the stream of consciousness, renderings of psychotic states – are none of them strictly innovations. Since the time of James Joyce they have been employed time and time again. They are common in contemporary American fiction, and have heavily influenced – and in turn been influenced by – the techniques of the cinema. None of this, however, can be said of the peculiar handling of the intractable material of *Two Thousand Seasons* which, to the reader conversant with modern naturalistic fiction, seems to mark an entirely new departure.

For these reasons, the initial critical reaction to the work on its first appearance was decidedly mixed. To start off with Armah clearly had some difficulty finding a publisher. When eventually it was published in East Africa, *The Daily Graphic*, one of Ghana's major daily newspapers, decided to call attention to this literary event and honour one of the now most celebrated of the nation's literati by serializing it in successive issues. Public reaction, however, was not good, and the serialization dried up after a few instalments. To this day the work remains comparatively unknown and unconsidered outside a small circle of those professionally concerned with African literature and, even there, the critical coverage it has received has been small.

All of these instances of resistance are in effect symptoms of the same underlying cause: a deep anxiety and puzzlement as to the novel's form. Indeed even the term 'novel', though it appears clearly on the title page, sits oddly on a book so apparently remote from existing novelistic models. Even in the context of contemporary African literature where formal dissension from the European fictional mode has been a key factor, the book looks decidedly odd. Wole Soyinka's difficult and convoluted study of urban *mœurs*, *The Interpreters*,[2] seems almost tame and conventional by comparison. It is not that the book is hermetic or difficult to understand. Indeed, it is by far the easiest of Armah's books to grasp, and complaints about its intellectual level are more likely to centre on the issue of banality. The problem is that it is so unlike anything which the general reader has ever approached before, that at times one is almost tempted to think of it as a 'chronicle' rather than a novel proper.

The question of nomenclature, however, is only significant in so far as it serves to attract our attention to a more seminal topic of debate: in what tradition, if any, is Armah here writing? Are we here confronted with a throw-back to the tradition of pure folk tale? Is Armah attempting something analogous to parable, or emanating from myth? Is the author trying to manufacture, or re-make, a body of legend, or is he pointing forward to some quite new, and as yet unperceived form? All of these possibilities crowd into the mind as one reads the story and tries, desperately at first, to 'place' the writing in some literary or oral current with which one has some familiarity.

There are, however, precedents for this kind of writing, though they are not easy to locate for readers whose literary experience is confined to the English language tradition. As we have already noted, Armah's intellectual allegiances are often more nearly akin to francophone writing than are those of most other writers from English-speaking Africa. The literary provenance of *Two Thousand Seasons* is a clear case in point. If one wishes to place it in any defined novelistic tradition, one has to look back into the history of recent French language fiction, and in particular at two works: André Schwartz-Bart's *Le Dernier des justes* (1959),[3] and the Malian novelist Yambo Ouologuem's notorious tour de force, *Le Devoir de violence* (1968).[4]

Literary Ancestry

André Schwartz-Bart's book, *Le Dernier des justes*, won – deservedly – the Prix Goncourt in 1959. It is an immense historical chronicle taking in several hundred years of European history and encapsulating the experience of the Jewish race from the early Middle Ages to the Second World War in a saga which takes them from the famous York massacre in the twelfth century to the gas-ovens of Auschwitz. The geographical breadth of the narrative is also impressive, following as it does one particular Jewish family from the North of England to France, Spain, Russia, Poland, Germany, back to France and then, finally, through deportation, back to Poland. Through all these migrations one central notion and hope binds the people together, the belief that in each generation God will provide for them a sacrificial, saintly, figure to bear the weight of their tribulation, one 'juste'. As the generations go by, we watch this sacred trust being carried on from individual to individual as gradually the will of Jaweh is made manifest. The pace of the narrative gradually slows down until we find ourselves in Poland at the outbreak of the First World War, where to a poor Yiddish couple is born a frail and querulous son, Ernie Lévy, the eponymous 'dernier des justes'. Ernie is in some ways a surprising heir to the tradition, and it is only gradually that his vocation reveals itself. We watch him grow up in a provincial German town against the growing threat of racial persecution and the increasing harassment of the Nazi authorities. Eventually, as war finally breaks out again, he is evacuated with his family to the outskirts of Paris, where he achieves momentary happiness with a crippled young Jewess named Golda, before he is induced to give himself up to the occupying forces of the Reich, and eventual extermination, by the news that his own parents have been incarcerated. Thus, at the very end, he fulfills his sacrificial function, becoming the last of the paschal line.

André Schwartz-Bart's is a moving and, despite the horrors of the circumstances that it describes, an in some ways idealistic book. Its theme is racial memory and the inherited trust of communal integrity. As such it is an unlikely progenitor of the next book in our series, Yambo Ouologuem's *Le Devoir de violence* published in 1968, when it won the coveted Prix Renaudot. Nevertheless, the links between the two books are well attested and, even if the second novel was not deliberately commissioned by the publishers, as has been claimed, as some sort of sequel, yet the affinities are many and not difficult to trace. To begin with, the two novels cover an approximately equivalent period, from the early Middle Ages to the middle of this century. The opening section heading of Ouologuem's work, 'La légende des Saifs', echoes the first chapter of Schwartz-Bart's, 'La légende des justes'. Both project the unitary notion of some sort of spiritual ancestry or principle running across the centuries. More importantly, though Yambo Ouologuem's volume is slimmer, the narrative shape of both books irresistibly recall one another. In both there is this opening headlong rush through the centuries, slowing down at some point shortly before the Second World War, when to an impoverished and obscure couple is born the son who will in some sense inherit the burden of his race's suffering, in the case of Ouologuem's book, one Raymond Spartacus. He comes, like Ernie Lévy, to Paris, where after an incongruously lyrical homosexual love affair with an Alsation by the name of Lambert, he is enticed back to his own country of Nakem and the unscrupulous hands of its rulers, the rapacious Saifs. Thus Ouologuem's work concludes with the supremacy of the named bearers of the 'legend', where Schwartz-Bart's ended with their extermination.

The different twist given to the endings of these two works in some sense distils the overriding difference to tone throughout. For though Raymond is, like Ernie in the earlier book, also quintessentially a victim, Ouologuem's narrative focus fastens not on these, the losers of history, but on the forces and agents of oppression. *Le Devoir de violence* is set in a legendary kingdom called Nakem, existing somewhere in the savannah and desert regions of the Western Sudan and owing, perhaps, some of its inspiration and detail to Ouologuem's own Dogon people. The history of this part of West Africa is portrayed as one long night of depravity, lust and oppression, presided over by its bizarre and venal overlords, the Saifs themselves, half-Negro, half- (*pace* Schwartz-Bart) Jew. By a process of systematic wheeling and dealing the Saifs have managed to maintain their grisly supremacy through various phases of political development (though the phrase is made to seem singularly inappropriate, since very little progresses): inter-tribal warfare; Arab domination; and finally French imperialism. At each stage, Saif technically succumbs, but in practice remains on top of the heap, dispatching in turn each of his enemies, from the inconvenient servant Sankolo to the lecherous French commandant, Chevalier. Saif proceeds through many incarnations and embodiments, and yet remains immutably the same. It is he who, for his own devious purposes, despatches Raymond Spartacus to France, for higher studies, yet he too who finally calls him back to assume the position of French deputy, in fact merely to act as his latest and most gullible instrument.

The tone of Ouologuem's book is thus predominantly dark, yet it is enlivened by snatches of grim humour, and under it all one senses the rumble of a hollow, satirical laughter. The basic question raised by the novel is not that of its literary genesis so much – too much paper has already been wasted on that score – as the problem of precisely placing that tone. Wole Soyinka has probably come closest to defining it when, in his critical work *Literature, Myth and the African World*, he comments:

> Is there a touch of self-hate in Ouologuem's 'dispassionate' recital? The intensity of contempt for the victims is clearly intended to reflect the alienation of the torturers from the concept of the victims as human, to reflect their religious-imperial justification for acts of barbarism, yet beneath this device there lurks, one suspects, the discomfort of the author himself. The epithets are spat through gritted teeth, the antidote for victim-identification appears to be a deflective masochism – Ouologuem has been accused of an alienation technique; the opposite seems truer – such a level of inventive degradation suggests that Ouologuem is practising some form of literary magic for the process of self-inoculation.[5]

Self-inoculation maybe, but Ouologuem's work was not addressed to himself, but to an audience whom he wishes to persuade. That he had a very special audience in mind became very obvious when, in the very next year, he published his open prose epistle, *Lettre à la France nègre*,[6] a spontaneous and explosive document in which he took the whole French-speaking world, black and white; to task for the besetting sin of Negro worship, the 'mauvaise conscience' which is so ungainly a cultural reaction from earlier colonial simplifications. The whole of this prose letter is in effect a set of variations on Fanon's well-known dictum that 'he who loves the negro is as sick as he who hates him', and an expanded comment on the phenomenon of historical distortion and over-idealization which he had, in *Le Devoir de violence* castigated under the name of 'Schrobeniusism'.

The point perhaps needs expanding a little. In any post-colonial state, the way that the future of the nation is envisaged is inextricably bound up with the particular construction put on the past. Given the fact that strict historical objectivity is impossible, the past of any country is liable to biased interpretations by those who wish to persuade the population to think of themselves in specific ways. In the nationalist, or early post-independence stage, the most tempting tendency will be to glorify the past so as to make up for the systematic denigration of it by the old imperial government. It was to this pressing danger that Wole Soyinka himself called the Nigerian people on the eve of their independence in his play *A Dance of the Forests* (1960).[7] Ouologuem too has recognized this danger, but instead of, as in Soyinka's play, establishing a mechanism for the redemption of the past, he has fallen prey to self-mockery, and, in an attempt to dissuade himself and others from this kind of over-simplification, has 'inoculated' himself with a heavy dose of cynicism so as to attain resistance to the prevailing bug.

But there is more than one way in which history may be distorted. Until recently European historians have been content to dismiss all of African history as a bottomless, and possibly unsavoury, abyss. The over-correction of this misunderstanding to which more recent African apologists have been prone may in itself constitute a vice: but it has been one of very short duration compared to the previous centuries of racist historical contempt. A polyglot intellectual of Ouologuem's stature may feel a need to inoculate himself against an over-compensating reaction, yet to the majority of his countrymen together with the beleagured masses of the Third World the fresh emphasis is still news. Ouologuem's enterprise only possesses cogency within the charmed circle of the over-informed: to the average reader his book is more likely to cause confusion, even anger.

It is to this neglected intellectual proletariat that Ayi Kwei Armah, a more democratic writer than the brilliant and waspish Mr Ouologuem, addresses his novel *Two Thousand Seasons*. Indeed almost the first thing one notes about it is that the audience at which the writing is aimed is envisaged very carefully. The third person, singular or plural, does not come easily to Armah's pen here, being more or less reserved for those with whom he is out of sympathy, the 'destroyers' or the 'predators'; nor has he much recourse to that constant stand-by of the 'romantic' Euro-pean artist, the first person singular. In fact, the verbal forms of the prose style in this book are reserved almost exclusively for first and second person plural:

> We are not a people of yesterday. Do they ask how many single seasons we have flowed from our beginnings till now? We shall point them to the proper beginning of their counting. (East African Publishing House, p. 1; Heinemann Educational Books, p. 1)

> You hearers, seers, imaginers, thinkers, rememberers, you prophets called to communicate truths of the living way to a people fascinated unto death, you called to link memory with forelistening, to join the uncountable seasons of our flowing to unknown tomorrows even more numerous, communicators doomed to pass on truths of your origins to a people rushing deathward, grown contemptuous in our ignorance of our source, prejudiced against our own survival, how shall your voca-tion's utterance be heard? (*Two Thousand Seasons*, EAPH, p. ix; Heinemann, p. ix)

By and large, the first person plural is used to denote the 'people', an entity synonymous with the book's audience, a group moreover with which the narrator strongly identifies. By implication, the writer further seems to claim membership of a more select group, the 'hearers' invoked by use of the second person plural in the second extract above. These 'hearers, seers, imaginers, thinkers' at first seem barely defined, until one recalls the fact that they possess a discernable ancestry in Armah's work, being none other than the 'lunatic seers' referred to in the long balcony passage from *The Beautyful Ones Are Not Yet Born* quoted at the end of Chapter 2 of this study. They form in effect a sort of revolutionary vanguard, and consist of all those whose gifts are predominantly artistic, spiritual, or intellectual. The relationship between these and the wider community, the 'we' of the text, is hence that between a responsible intellectual élite and the mass towards whom their whole obligation lies. This relationship is conceived of as being direct and vital, in contrast to Armah's previous works, where it is seen as impervious and moribund.

The culminating impression of all three of Armah's earlier novels was that of an immense and irredeemable loneliness. The tortured and self-aware artist, unable to communicate either his ideals or his creations, dwelt in an intense and brooding void. The primary reason for this is that, in those books, the artist figure was conceived in entirely European terms. Though fired with a sense of social mission, in practice he was as cut off from the rest of the community as Byron's Childe Harold or Goethe's Werther. Solo in *Why Are We So Blest?* and Baako in *Fragments* are both heirs to the nineteenth-century Romantic tradition of artistic isolation. In *Two Thousand Seasons* Armah has resolved this difficulty by envisaging the social contact of the artist in terms more appropriate to a traditional African community. The 'hearers, seers, imaginers, thinkers' form in effect a class of griots, poet-historians whose vision of their role has far more in common with that of the Yoruba Ijala singer or Ewe lyricist that with the self-conscious *angst* of many a Western artist. That even they are perceived as living in relative isolation – the sacred groves beyond the clan's confines – is no reflection of the way in which they view themselves, but simply a measure of the advanced process of dissolution to which the community itself is portrayed as having been exposed during the core of the narrative.

To each artistic tradition there pertains, not only a social role, but also a distinctive mode of expression. The European novelist until compara-tively recently tended to approach his material by means of a consecutive, naturalistic story line. There are exceptions to this – and in this century the tradition has, as we have already noted, been subject to certain modifications – yet the basic orientation remains constant, the author's country being plot, character, theme and situation.[8] To traditional African artists such as the Senegalese griot, for example, most of these technical devices are profoundly alien. He deals, not with a realistic story line held tightly in the dimensions of time and space, but with the longer perspectives of legend and myth. This is not to say that his visions are any less true than those of his European counterpart: in fact, in one sense, they are truer, since his emanations have less to do with the Imagination in Coleridge's sense of the word,[9] than with the communal memory, a certain conception of history.

Both André Schwartz-Bart's *Le Dernier des justes* and Yambo Ouologuem's *Le Devoir de violence* are, in some sense, historical works. Yet Schwarz-Bart's work is decidedly a product of the conscious imagination; Ouologuem's, to keep Coleridge's terminology, a product of the acrobatic fancy. Ouologuem tosses up facts, names, rumours and the occasional outrageous invention with the dexterity and self-mocking charm of an extravagant juggler. There is a certain glibness about his novel, and the level of his seriousness is constantly suspect. None of this can be said of Armah, whose fourth novel, deeply committed to its subject matter as it is, provides us with an instance of *littérature engagée* at its most earnest. Yet it owes nothing to the modern existentialist mode of writing, being attuned to something much older, far more grounded in the realities with which it deals, the plural voice of the traditional artist, whose instruments are myth, legend, folk-tale and proverb.

There are several African novelists who have attempted to integrate folklore material into their books. The story of the tortoise and the birds in Chapter 11 of Chinua Achebe's *Things Fall Apart*[10] is a case in point, as is the use of proverb in both that novel and *Arrow of God*.[11] Yet precious few of them have attempted to structure a whole work around certain key myths. One exception would be the various embodiments of the Yoruba pantheon that make up the artist Kola's canvas in Wole Soyinka's *The Interpreters*. Yet even here the mythological framework is set off against the satirical flow of a lively naturalistic narrative. In *Two Thousand Seasons*, however, we are confronted with myth in a raw, compelling shape. Specifically, Armah has drawn on two legendary sources. The historical experience of the whole African people from the dawn of remembered history to the present day has been localized in terms of the migrations and tribulations of the Akan people, which over the centuries have brought them from the fabled glories of the early mediaeval Sudanic empires to the forest and coastal settlements which are their present abode. This source of inspiration, part recorded history, part myth, has an appealing epic shape to it, which serves to suggest the ample motions of historical development. The specific claim of an historical origin in the Western Sudan has great cogency: powerfully employed by J. B. Danquah in the 1940s as a rallying point for nationalist agitation, it was the major reason why the modern nation state of Ghana was given the same name as the tenth-century African empire described by Arabic Chroniclers. It has already provided the imaginative framework for one work of literature: Edward Braithwaite's epic poem of historical confrontation, *Masks*.[12] The other myth upon which Armah draws here is the story of Anoa, the young Akan girl, granted disturbing reveries of the future enslavement of her people, visions which she in vain attempted to communicate to a complacent populace. This again is a legend of immense poetic force which has also inspired a previous off-shoot: the play *Anoa*[13] by Armah's contemporary and compatriot Ama Atta Aidoo.

The Text

It is the opening prelude of *Two Thousand Seasons* which sets the tone. In its evocation of endlessly shifting time, it is very like the first section of *Fragments*, 'Naana', only here the motion is, if anything, even less definite. An impression is created of vast numinous forces moving in an opaque and drifting mist, with only the sensation of continual, intermittent conflict to give direction to the whole. The 'drugged somnambulistic flow' which Gerald Moore finds to be characteristic of Armah's prose style here reaches its apotheosis, and though, as Wole Soyinka notes, the writing at this point occasionally 'creaks',[14] the aesthetic impact is undeniable. It is also, significantly, here that the connection posited in the first chapter of this study between Armah's prose style and his conception of history becomes most evident, the ambling pace of the sentences evoking a circular notion of time. The emphasis, however, does not stop short at evocation: essentially this opening prolegomenon or preface constitutes a kind of appeal or apostrophe to the toiling millions who have borne the brunt of history's oppression, and to the 'hearers, seers' who are their spokesmen. The entire purport of this kind of artistic project thus becomes clear: a purpose not exhausted by narrative or description, but proceeding to prescription and prognosis:

> Would you lock your gift away in pallid silence? Know then that in the absence of the utterers' work the carnage will be long and pure and not the wisest mind can in the absence of the utterers' work trace in all our flowing blood even one broken ring of meaning. For those returning, salvaging blistered selves from death, and those advancing still hypnotized by death, in the absence of the utterers' work what will they be but beasts devouring beasts, zombis fighting zombis, a continuation along the road of death in place of regeneration, the rediscovery of our way, the way? (EAPH, pp. xvii–xviii; Heinemann, p. xv)

The prelude also introduces us to the work's main image patterns. The first and most prominent of these is the image of springwater flowing into an endless desert in which it is parched to the point of extinction. The idea clearly has geographical pertinence in view of the many Northwards-flowing tributaries of the rivers Niger and Volta: its rationale, however, does not originate in climatology. In order to detect the source of this symbolism we have to look back to Armah's first novel, *The Beautyful Ones Are Not Yet Born*, in which the idea of a persistent current, woefully polluted at its wellspring, despite its constant efforts to clear itself, is envisaged in a powerful passage in Chapter 3, quoted at the end of the second chapter of this study. The implication is the same in both instances, the stream serving to represent the original integral thrust of a united people, the elements of pollution, here the sand, clearly standing for the historical factors which compromise that. In *Two Thousand Seasons*, however, the element of sand is inextricably intertwined with another interlocking image pattern, that of colour.

Two Thousand Seasons is a book set in stark monochrome. Gone are the milling shades of the earlier books: the tinctures and tints that come from a mellow vision. By contrast we are here presented with two colours: black and white. It is pointless, I think, to beat about the bush by talking of racial 'overtones'. This is not a novel which deals in harmonics of any order, but in an overriding central melody. Black clearly stands for the African people: that is bold and unambiguous; white for all those forces which have over the centuries crushed and repressed them, be they Arab/Muslim, or European/Christian. Armah's point is that the effect, and much of the technique was the same; both groups are therefore represented by the single colour white, the white of parched sand.

It is here – at the outset – that many of Armah's readers will lodge a fundamental objection. It will be said that this novel is evidently racialist, and therefore, as art, invalid. The first part of that claim strikes me as true; the rest here not to follow from it. That Mr Armah's point is a racial one there can be no doubt. In the context of a naturalistic narrative, such divisiveness is evidently a decisive flaw, and hence must be criticized. In the account of *Why Are We So Blest?* already given we saw how the restriction of sympathy allotted to the white characters had the effect of overbalancing the work. In an artistic enterprise where one expects a rich ambivalence or generosity, such willful blinkering strikes one immediately as unacceptable. In *Two Thousand Seasons*, on the other hand, these objections do not apply, for the paradoxical reason that Armah carries his condemnation that little bit further, so that it no longer occupies the domain of realist art. We are in an altogether different terrain now, that appropriate to myth, legend, and racial memory. Ambivalence is not to be expected because we have transcended it, have either surmounted or side-stepped its possibilities in the necessary effort to provide a strong, healing mythology.

We have already noted that Armah's art possesses a strongly curative aspect: the comparison with medication is one which naturally occurs. 'See the disease, and understand it well', decrees the seer Isanusi at the end of *Two Thousand Seasons* (EAPH, p. 314; Heinemann, p. 201); we might add that the entirety of the novel itself provides a contribution to that undertaking. Armah has addressed his work unambiguously to a certain audience, the throng of the oppressed, the victims of the historical processes which he is elucidating. The object is to provide self-illumination – since to understand one's past is necessarily to understand at least part of oneself – and, through it, therapy. In the context of the massive communal inferiority complex described in the first chapter of this study, there is only one antidote, a heightening of self-respect, and we need fear no over-dosage. Armah's concern is to provide an overwhelming counteraction to the colonialist distortion of history. If, in the process, individuals other than the patients themselves are slighted, this has to be accepted: indeed, the wholesale condemnation of certain groups or classes is clearly permissible if from it there results an access of health and hope for those languishing under such a corrosive misunderstanding and mistrust of their own past. It is thus that the incidental exaggerations of the work justify themselves, as part of what, in a clinching phrase, Soyinka called 'the visionary reconstruction of the past for the purposes of social direction'.[15]

Despite the explicit racial logic of the work, it is important not to over-simplify by interpreting it in terms of a straightfoward distinction between indigenous virtue and foreign vice. While it remains true that the narrative edge cuts mercilessly against all extraneous influences, the cause of the initial disruption of the people's original cohesion is firmly located within the community itself. Against the natural and steadying social norm – 'our way, the way' – are pitted, from the outset, the disorganizing forces of greed and cupidity. These become manifest well before the arrival of the Arabs at the beginning of Chapter 2. Their first appearance coincides with a dislocation of the essential reciprocity of the marital relationship. Women, at first partners in the family enterprise, come increasingly to be regarded as servants, later to be used as mere objects, vehicles for utility and pleasure:

> The men, at length announcing a necessity to nurse their strength for the work of elephants, with the magic of words made weightier with furrowed brows successfully pulled themselves out of all ongoing

work, leaving only phantom heroic work, work which never found them, while generously they welcomed the women into all real work, proclaiming between calabashes of sweet ahey how obvious it was that all such work was of its nature trivial, easy, light and therefore far from a burden on any woman.

The peace of that fertile time spread itself so long, there was such an abundance of every provision, anxiety flew so far from us, that men were able to withdraw from even those unusual jobs they claimed they were holding themselves ready for, and their absence left no pain. They had elected to go with the women every farming day to sit in shady places guarding against danger. Danger came seldom. Pleading boredom the men replaced the shady places on the farm with shades closer home, next to the fragrant breweries of ahey. After this, even on those rare occasions when such work as the men had named their work happened, there were no men in sight.

The women were maintainers, the women were their own protec-tresses, finders and growers both. The lost exile seeking an end to his loneliness in rape out on the open farms; the huge python blindly spreading the terror gripping it in sudden discovery; the cat of the fields hunting unusual food; the maddened elephant; every danger the women tamed, bringing tales and skins and meat home to triumphant husbands. (EAPH, pp. 15–16; Heinemann, pp. 10–11)

It is this growing imbalance within the social texture of the tribe which stimulates the young prophetess Anoa into her forecast of two thousand seasons of spiritual and physical enslavement, an intimation based on her estimate of the people's present state of mind:

Reciprocity, that is the way you have forgotten, the giving, the receiv-ing, the living alternation of the way. The offerers, those givers who do not receive, they are mere victims. That is what in the heedless generosity of your blinding abundance you have turned yourselves into. (EAPH, p. 26; Heinemann, p. 17)

It is this pronouncement which issues in the major historical sweep of the work: a vast dipping span of a thousand years, consisting of a thousand seasons of increasing enslavement followed by a thousand seasons of resistance, which, in accordance with the method of calendar computa-tion adopted in the book – wet season, dry season, wet season and so on – gives us exactly the millenium between the people's first encounter with alien forces and their eventual reinstatement. The inception of this process is not so much the arrival of the Muslim overlords, as the abject manner in which they are welcomed by those elements already estranged from the communal life of the people.

Here too lay the beginning of our long bafflement at the heavy phenomenon of the slave forever conditioned against himself, against our people. With such never will there be any possibility of creation, never will new communities of the way be born within their presence. Such contain even in times of liberation's sweetest possibility an undying nostalgia for the worst times of the oppressors' domination over us, the times of suffering for the shattered community, because for such those are times of ease, times of prestige, times of privilege. To such the possibility itself of our liberation is a threat. Their lives in times of such possibility are long nightmares about their personal, precipitate descent from privilege. The events of our hope are to them real terrors. In their drugged moments of forgetfulness they dream of days when they were elevated slaves, not ordinary persons holding their own lives, their own futures together with our people. (EAPH, p. 42; Heinemann, p. 26)

After the arrival of the Arabs, this penchant for dependence reveals itself in evident and alarming ways, the major impact taking place within the social structure of the tribe itself. No model of African political stratification is actually proposed in the work, but the implied suggestion is that, in the first instance, all power and responsibility was shared, status groups as such being unknown. The social scientist might well find this naïve, yet it does serve as a hypothetical extreme pole to the institution of privileged kingship which the community develops under the tutelage of a foreign heirarchy. Kingship is here presented as an institution utterly alien to indigenous ways of thinking, a form of ascendancy immediately appealing to those who, like the idiot Koranche, are unable to sustain self-respect within the mutually rewarding give-and-take of normal social interaction. It is true that chieftancy, as understood and encouraged by Lugard-inspired British imperialists, was unknown to certain African ethnic groups before the colonial period, the Igbo people being a notable case in point. The importance of this absolute polarity between alternative political systems lies, however, not in any supposed fidelity to anthropological fact, but in the analysis it provides of the emergence of certain oppressive power groups, the way that they form, the mentality that they encourage and the debilitating habits they induce within the body politic. Armah's analysis of kingship substantially anticipates his understanding of the colonial and neo-colonial élites, both of which are held as being largely implicit within the pre-colonial set-up.

Colonialism proper, however, is not itself far off. In an effort to evade the disastrous clutches of the Arab 'predators', the people migrate downwards through the savannah region, into the rain forest and then on to the coast. Their efforts prove vain, since on their arrival they discover that they have walked into the hands of a foe far deadlier than the first, the Europeans with their guns, guile and seductive material enticements. It is predictably the king who is the first to succumb:

From the white missionary a message came. It said it was an incon-
trovertible teaching of the white religion that a king had a right, a duty
in fact, to impose his will strongly on his people, for to the white men
the king was always the head, the people merely the body. Replied the
king: I do not have the strength. Said the white trader: We can help
with that if you will be a faithful friend of ours, for that is what friends
are for. The king said secretly: Yes, but let us act in secret. And the
missionary spoke the final word in his message: Secrecy, yes, at the
appropriate time. But sometimes you the head will have to make
the heaviness of your authority felt, and felt openly. As for strength to
do it, fear nothing as long as you keep faith with us, your friends. The
strength of your friends is your strength also, as long as you take good
care to keep our friendship. (EAPH, p. 155; Heinemann, p. 99)

The complicity between the commercial interest, herald of a future
colonial administration, and the indigenous leadership thus supplies us,
not merely with an understanding of the mechanics of imperialism itself,
but also with a glimpse of the combination of spiritual and secular
leverage which was the Africans' undoing. For this sort of inducement
works to distort the matrix of social relationship at every level: organiza-
tional, religious, even personal. It is this last twist to the knife which
finally sets off the resistance campaign. At the point when Koranche
starts to use his secular power to force the hand of the unwilling Abena, it
is time for the committed younger members of the clan to take the
challenge up, spear-headed by the older, yet still defiant seer, Isanusi. In
the customary 'dance of love' – the dance of marital selection which
marks the end of puberty – the members of that year's age grade deliberately choose to link themselves together into a corporate grouping,
avoiding the closer involvement of pairing, so as the better to prepare
themselves for the task of liberation that lies ahead. Thereafter, they
retreat to the groves of initiation for a period of apprenticeship, forming
themselves under Isanusi's guidance into a close-knit revolutionary
cabal, a kind of embryonic Maquis ready to purge their society's growing
injustices. Their eager-eyed naïvety, however, proves their undoing,
since it is not long before they are tricked into slavery by the corrupt
collaboration of Koranche and his white mentors. Lured to the coast,
they are clapped into irons, despatched on board ship and, after a brief
detention in one of the coastal forts (it could be Cape Coast, or more
probably Elmina) for the purpose of branding, are sent out on the long
and gruesome middle passage to the Americas.

The story of the prisoners' transportation and eventual escape is
perhaps the weakest part of the work. It is here that the necessary
divisiveness of moral vision forces the characters into two irreconcilable
camps, according to a simple formula: black = good; white = bad. As

such we may justify the simplification as part of the total healing
enterprise: yet, when combined with the element of combativeness and
scheming, the resulting narrative texture has much in common with a
cops-and-robbers episode, or a saga of cowboys and indians. As Wole
Soyinka has also noted, 'This weakness often tends to make the book
read like an adventure story.'[16] We might add that this is the inevitable
result of slinging a fictional work around a straightforward Manichean
metaphysical divide: it is a fault strangely that one finds repeated in one
of Soyinka's own works, his second novel, *Season of Anomy*.[17]

Yet to say this is not to account entirely for the episode. The emphasis,
after all, is not so much on the facts of the plot as on the interpretation of
those facts. What enables the blacks to break free against such fantastic
odds? The answer to this question is intimately related to the whole
conceptual fabric of the work. It is something to do with a vestigial unity
of spirit, a survival from the lost 'reciprocity' that the worst efforts of the
traders cannot destroy. Armah gives it the term 'connectedness', and it
will prove instructive to contrast his description of it with the discovery
of something not dissimilar among the shackled slaves in that other saga
of transportation, Alex Haley's *Roots*.

Here is Haley's description of the moment at which his slaves happen
on the possibilities of inter-linguistic penetration:

> The steady murmuring that went on in the hold whenever the toubab
> were gone kept growing in volume and intensity as the men began to
> communicate better and better with one another. Words not under-
> stood were whispered from mouth to ear along the shelves until
> someone who knew more than one tongue would send back their
> meanings. In the process, all of the men along the shelf learned new
> words in tongues they had not spoken before. Sometimes men jerked
> upward, bumping their heads, in the double excitement of com-
> municating with each other and the fact that it was being done without
> the toubab's knowledge. Muttering among themselves for hours, the
> men developed a deepening sense of intrigue and of brotherhood.
> Though they were of different villages and tribes, the feeling grew that
> they were not from different people or places.[18]

Here, by contrast, is Armah:

> Of unconnected consciousness is there more to say beyond the clear
> recognition this is destruction's keenest tool against the soul? That the
> left hand should be kept ignorant of what its right twin is made to do –
> who does not see in that cleavage the prime success of the white
> destroyers' road of death? That the heart detached should beat no
> faster even when limbs familiar to it are moved to heinous acts – is that
> not already the severed atrophy of connected faculties, the white
> method of destruction? That our left eye should be set to see against its
> twin, not with it – surely that is part of the white destroyers' two

thousand seasons of triumph against us? (EAPH, pp. 200–1; Heinemann, p. 128)

Granted that Haley is writing firmly within the convention of naturalistic narrative, while Armah is engaged in the construction of myth, the drift of Armah's prose here provides us, not only with a philosophical context in which to view the ensuing action, but furthermore a whole critique of a certain civilization.

A marked interpretational thrust also illuminates the next phase of the story: the return to Anoa and a rearguard campaign against the forces of complicity in the by now severely compromised community. Armah's attention is here focused on the weak spots implicit in any such project, the areas of sensitivity in the under-belly of the committed, unsteeled by resolve. Explicitly it is a longing for family life, and a simple clannish tenderness, that drives those such as the sentimental Dovi back into the bosom of a corrupted society, leading eventually to his betrayal of the cause and of his former associates. The case of kinship does not appeal only to him – hardly a member of the beleaguered group of rebels fails to feel the seductive pull. Yet, so the implication goes, it is an attraction that must be resisted at all costs if the insurgents are to retain any integrity of purpose. One remembers in this connection Teacher, the solitary seer of *The Beautyful Ones Are Not Yet Born*, and his stout resistance of the claims of the 'loved ones', which have so wretchedly undermined the purposefulness of his friend, the man. One finds here then further evidence of the consistency of thinking in all Armah's output, which, despite a hefty shift in novelistic method, has retained his grasp on certain salient tenets of analysis and belief.

Increasingly, towards the end, though the historical period envisaged is presumably comparatively remote, the situations described appear to be contemporary. The megolomaniac Kamuzu, for instance, whom the rebels unwittingly back as a counterweight to the white 'destroyers', and who in style and mannerism seems to belong to the late eighteenth century, comes to represent a sort of stereotype of modern neo-colonialist dictatorship, such as that associated with the last days of Nkrumah. This is especially evident in his fondness for the mere symbolism of power:

> What spurious praise names did we not invent to lull Kamuzu's buffoon spirit?
> > Osagyefo!
> > Kantamanto!
> > Kabiyesi!
> > Sese!
> > Mwenyenguvu!

Otumfuo!
Dishonest words are the food of rotten spirits.
We filled Kamuzu to bursting with his beloved nourishment. (EAPH,
p. 267; Heinemann, p. 171)

The sustained and on-going guerrilla campaign, moreover, with which
the book ends, has much more in common with the small-unit scale of
recent terrorist warfare than the drilled, flag-waving nature of earlier
colonial conflicts. Indeed what seems to be envisaged is a prolonged civil
war, a sustained campaign to purify national life of undesirable elements,
rather than an attack waged on any external foe. Is Armah then advocat-
ing violence within the modern African nation state? One strongly
worded passage would seem to negate this construction:

We do not utter praise of arms. The praise of arms is the praise of
things, and what shall we call the soul crawling so low, soul so hollow it
finds fulfilment in the praising of mere things? It is not things we praise
in our utterance, not arms we praise but the living relationship itself of
those united in the use of all things against the white sway of death, for
creation's life. (EAPH, p. 320; Heinemann, p. 205)

The emphasis here as throughout the closing pages is on the necessary
effort to rid the culture of its debilitating material dependence on 'things'
– objects valued for their own sake – and on the international community
which provides them. The antidote is not primarily bloodshed – though
certainly the phrasing does not exclude that – but an access of confidence
and the creative security that comes from cultural assertion. A necessary
concomitant of this process is a wilful damaging of the image and prestige
of those who, by their financial and political influence, inevitably impede
this kind of national growth. It is in this context that the concluding call
to arms has to be seen, as an extended metaphor for the cultivation of
self-understanding and the autonomy of social and artistic life.

The very last paragraph of the text conjures up a glowing picture of an
infinitely receding and glorious future:

Against this what a vision of creation yet unknown, higher, much more
profound than all erstwhile creation! What a hearing of the confluence
of all the waters of life flowing to overwhelm the ashen desert's blight!
What an utterance of the coming together of all the people of our way,
the coming together of all people of the way. (EAPH, p. 321;
Heinemann, p. 206)

Thus the central image of dammed and clotted headwaters, which has
been used all along to suggest the inhibition of natural health and
progress, finally accumulates to power a vision of a destiny strong in
resilience and self-reliance. There is nothing naïve in this conclusion,

nothing to contradict the mournfulness of the opening passages, for example, since all the qualifications and reservations have already been put. The brisk confidence and optimism of this close does, however, serve to readjust the impression of the much commented on 'disillusionment' in Armah's earlier writing, or rather help us to see it for what it is, a sad recognition of the distance that the evolving national spirit has still to go. The 'beautyful ones' may not yet be born, but the seed is already firmly planted in the soil, if only the waters of the people's neglected genius would combine to water it.

The end of the book also serves to contest impressively the bleak version of African history presented by Yambo Ouologuem in his earlier work. Whether or not *Two Thousand Seasons* was deliberately written as an answer to *Le Devoir de violence* – and, going on internal evidence, there would seem to be some justification for saying that it was – the heartening tone of voice with which it concludes, and the democratic appeal which pervades the whole, goes a long way to negate Ouologuem's cynicism. It is thus nonsensical, despite the formal similarities in the two books, to credit them with the same point of view, or, as at least one commentator has done, to see them as exemplifying the same novelistic tendency:

> The contemporary novel in Africa seems to be locked in an agonized search for a vision of political excellence on that continent. But this is merely a reflection of the social realities of the politics of Africa. Perhaps the African novelist has not yet been able to break from the cycle of angst and frustration. The Malian novelist Yambo Ouologuem and the Ghanaian novelist Ayi Kwei Armah seem to epitomize this era of intense despair.[19]

In order to correct this sort of critical short-sightedness, a cursory glance at *Two Thousand Seasons*, extended by a patient and careful rereading of the earlier books, is all that is needed.

REFERENCES AND NOTES

1. Ayi Kwei Armah, *Two Thousand Seasons* (Nairobi: East African Publishing House, 1973; London: Heinemann Educational Books, 1979). Page references in the text are given for both editions.
2. Wole Soyinka, *The Interpreters* (London: Heinemann Educational Books, 1970).
3. André Schwartz-Bart, *Le Dernier des justes* (Paris: Editions du Seuil, 1959).
4. Yambo Ouologuem, *Le Devoir de violence* (Paris: Editions du Seuil, 1968).
5. Wole Soyinka, *Literature, Myth and the African World* (Cambridge: Cambridge University Press, 1976), p. 101.
6. Yambo Ouologuem, *Lettre à la France nègre* (Paris: Éditions Edmond Nalis, 1969).
7. Wole Soyinka, *A Dance of Forests* (Oxford: Oxford University Press, 1963).
8. See, for instance, the account of the form given in E. M. Forster's *Aspects of the Novel* (London: Edward Arnold, 1937; Harmondsworth: Penguin Books, 1970).

9. See S. T. Coleridge, *Biographia Literaria* (London: Dent, 1967), Chapter XIII, p. 167.

10. Chinua Achebe, *Things Fall Apart* (London: Heinemann Educational Books, 1971).

11. Chinua Achebe, *Arrow of God* (London: Heinemann Educational Books, 1966).

12. From Edward Braithwaite, *The Arrivants: A New World Trilogy* (Oxford: Oxford University Press, 1973).

13. Ama Atta Aidoo, *Anoa* (Harlow: Longman, 1970).

14. Soyinka, *Literature, Myth and the African World*, *op. cit.*, p. 114.

15. Soyinka, ibid., p. 106.

16. Soyinka, *Literature, Myth and the African World*, *op. cit.*, p. 114.

17. Wole Soyinka, *Season of Anomy* (London: R. Collings, 1973).

18. Alex Haley, *Roots* (London: Hutchinson, 1977), p. 168.

19. Kofi Awoonor, *The Bread of the Earth* (New York: Doubleday, 1975), p. 304.

6 The Healers

▼▼▼▼▼▼▼▼▼▼▼▼▼▼▼▼▼▼▼▼▼▼▼▼▼▼▼▼▼▼

*T*HE *Healers*[1] is the first of Armah's novels to bear the categorical sub-heading 'an historical novel'. If the drift of our argument has been followed through the analysis of the successive stages of his work, it may be thought that the genre is largely implicit in most of his books. After all, *Two Thousand Seasons*, as we have just seen, is a novel which takes it upon itself to interpret a vast span of a thousand years according to a certain point of view, yet that was simply subtitled 'a novel'. While Armah's first three books may not at any point actively invoke the remoter past, yet chronology is very relevant to their understanding. Each of them is vividly redolent of a particular period of time, albeit a recent one: the mid-1960s. Apart from this historical placing, there is, particularly in the imagery of *The Beautyful Ones*, a powerful sense of an added long perspective which, acting as a back-drop to the events described, serves to give them a certain depth. They are then, in these senses at least, historical novels. Despite all this, I think that most readers would quibble about applying this rather special label to them, while feeling that, in the case of Armah's latest book, such a classification is more than justified. What is it, then, about *The Healers* that sets it apart?

Like *Two Thousand Seasons*, *The Healers* is a book with an implicit but definable purpose. The strength of the former novel lies in the way in which it directly challenges the distorted view of African history conventionally put about by earlier European scholars – abetted to a certain extent by such indigenous sophisticates as Yambo Ouologuem – and, in so doing, attempts to cure its African readership of the acute inherited self-distrust under which many of them labour. Like most of Armah's books, but more boldly so, it is a therapeutic work which aims to close the wounds left over and festering from centuries of implied cultural abuse. *The Healers* too is germane to this enterprise – indeed its very title suggests a propensity to cure. In *Two Thousand Seasons*, however, the very breadth of the canvas employed of necessity involved a weakening of the design at certain points; in between sharp, telling brushstrokes, there were patches of dull or diluted colour intended to cover over stretches where the adumbration of detail would have been irrelevant or repetitive.

This is hardly surprising: history, viewed in this light, may consist of
a process of cultural confrontation, but the conflict, while ongoing, cannot be equally intense at each moment. At certain junctures the forces
which lie dormant over long periods erupt, producing a dramatic and
exciting effect: it is here that the novelist can home in and arrest the
reader's attention with a burst of action, a visible disturbance of historical
terrain.

The Healers concentrates on just such a moment. While Armah's
novelistic method precludes the exact enumeration of dates, a series of
clues dropped near the beginning of the text enables us to fix the action
precisely in both time and place. For instance, a passage very near to the
inception of the story warns against historical vagueness:

> Did you remember to tell your listeners of what time, what age you
> rushed so fast to speak? Or did you leave the listener floundering in
> endless time, abandoned to suppose your story belonged to any confus-
> ing age? Is it a story of yesterday, or is it of last year? Is it from the time
> of the poet Nyankoman Dua, seven centuries ago? Or did it take place
> ten centuries ago, when Ghana was not just a memory, and the
> eloquent ones before you still sang praises to the spirit holding
> our people together? Is it of that marvellous black time before the
> desert was turned desert, thirty centuries and more ago? Or have you
> let the listener know the truth: that this story now is not so old – just
> over a century old? (EAPH, p. 3; Heinemann Educational Books,
> p. 2)

This paragraph helps the reader to get his bearings in more than one
respect. He learns not only to place the story somewhere in the late
nineteenth century, not merely in Ghana, real rather than fabled, but also
once again in the region of the Akan people who featured so prominently
in *Two Thousand Seasons*. Whereas, however, in the previous novel, he
was expected to take the history of the Akan as indicative of the fortunes
of the whole black race, here he is led to understand that he is dealing
with the real territorially defined Akan tribe or, more precisely still, the
Asante empire at a certain stage in its development. That he should be
able to place himself imaginatively at this exact point of Asante history is
far more important than merely being able to read off the events
described against the European calendar. For this reason instead of
conventional dates he is given a whole series of clues which enable him to
conjure up the precise historical moment in terms derived from the local
culture itself.

The Asante, he learns, are poised at a point of maximum expansion.
Having already put down their Denchira neighbours, they are intensifying their constant skirmishes with the Fante to the south. Indeed he soon
discovers that a whole column has been dispatched to harass settlements

on the coast – Amankwa Tia off to claim Elmina. Though the imperial
hierarchy is, at least at the outset, firmly in control, there has apparently
been a recent change at the apex of the structure, and Kofi Karikari, the
new Asantehene, is having trouble restraining certain dissident elements
among the aristocracy.

The exactitude of these details is augmented by certain broader perspectives. The culture to which the reader is introduced is a slaving
society, monolithic, exuberant, by turns aggressive or self-doubting,
attuned to trade and tribute as a means both of sustenance and
supremacy. Technically, though adept, it is vulnerable, since certain of
the advantages of industrialized Europe have passed it by. During the
series of martial contests in which the young men compete at the beginning of the book 'the ancient hunting tools – arrows, spears, knives –
were not to be used. Ages had passed since the gun had replaced them.'
(EAPH, p. 52; Heinemann, p. 42). Firearms then are a firmly established
part of the military scene, though when confronted with a Rait's gun
towards the end of the novel, the Asante messengers evince despair and
an almost superstitious awe. All of these facts enable us to locate the
action of the novel at a minutely exact point in history, in fact during the
years 1873 and 1874, during what historians have come to know as
the Second Asante War.

It should be evident that the extent of this historical placing is intended
in no sense here as elaboration. It is, among other things, one way of
signalling to those readers familiar with the novel immediately prior to
this that the method of approach here is fundamentally different. Above
all, historicity is here to be viewed, not as an eternally flowing stream, or
an endlessly repetitive cycle, but rather as a multi-layered texture whose
subtler depths may best be plumbed by inserting the narrative instrument at one precise point; the more precise the more accurate the
findings. To put it another way, the historical method in *Two Thousand
Seasons* was deductive. Starting from certain clearly defined tenets or
premises, it set out to establish their relevance, taking the entire span of
the racial memory as its example. *The Healers*, on the other hand, may be
viewed as an inductive work. Taking as its field of inquiry a particular
moment when the stresses to which one society was habitually subject
arose to overwhelm it, it sets out to demonstrate the reasons for this
failure and hence to illustrate something about the nature, not only of this
culture, but perhaps also of all comparable societies which succumb to
external pressure in this way. It thus tells us something very important
about the whole colonial experience. At the heart of the novel there lies an
overriding question: why were the immensely proud and resourceful
Asante people subjected in this ignoble manner? In answering it, the

novel helps us to understand some basic truths about the social interaction of different and hostile cultures. For all these reasons, the term 'historical novel' seems far more appropriate than it does in the case of any of Armah's earlier books.

The historical episode on which Armah chooses to concentrate is one which has been subject to a peculiar amount of misrepresentation by European historians. Seen from the Western point of view, the history of the late nineteenth century has often been seen as a process of rapid expansion of colonial frontiers, the bringing of the light to 'darkest Africa' being but a benign offshoot of this development. In this scenario the final humiliation of a remote African people during the Second Asante War features as a minor, though piquant peccadillo, an obscure and often ignored sub-paragraph in school textbooks. It is true that recent historians, many of them African, have to a certain extent re-educated scholarly opinion in this matter, and that in recent studies of this episode the tendency has increasingly been to concentrate on the internal politics of the Asante empire. Despite this, in the popular mind the overwhelming impression persists of an incident that was both fitting and inevitable, the irresistable impact of a technically superior force on a bewildered but headstrong people stuck in a cultural backwater. The sad fact is that this notion not only retains its hold over the minds of most people in the West, but, thanks to the importation of metropolitan ideas through the colonial educational system, has come to determine the way that some Africans regard their own history.

It is this state of affairs which Armah takes it upon himself to challenge. The book is thus not merely a reinstatement of a neglected and misunderstood phase of the colonial past, but part of the total reclamation of history on behalf of those whose contribution received opinion has traditionally slighted or abused. In attempting to achieve this Armah has availed himself of all the latest advances in the field: the novel shows abundant evidence of extensive research, and a subtle appreciation of the various factors involved in a complex historical issue. Yet his attitude to established fact is far from slavish. Armah is a novelist, not an academic historian, and, in time honoured fashion, he has used and shaped the available material so as to tailor history to a particular vision. There is nothing odd or underhand about this, and it accords with long established precedent. Shakespeare relied for his English history plays on sources which distorted the mediaeval Wars of the Roses, thus producing a version flattering to the Tudor dynasty. So Armah, in pursuit of his ideal of spiritual health, has used history as a medicine for rankling sores, and hence acted as a healer of his own people. It is important to realize that his purpose, however, has not been simply to dull the pain; as well as the soothing salve he has also applied in several places the rack, since to cure one has often to cause pain.

What are the crucial weaknesses of Asante society as portrayed in the book? Despite a superficial solidarity it is gradually revealed as a culture barely at ease with itself. Bent as it is on physical conquest of its neighbours, it obviously prizes the martial arts highly. This can be seen in the series of contests at the beginning of the book in which the heir apparent to the Esuono throne, Appia, has to hold his own in a range of trials of strength and wit against his contemporaries: in wrestling, target-practice, and oware (a game of skill involving the capture of the opponent's position by spilling dried seeds into two parallel lines of holes). The winner will obtain immense social prestige; and this again tells us something very important about the Asante. Despite the system of aristocratic inheritance, great stress is placed on the element of competition and personal excellence. The system of ascribed hereditary status is hence subject to certain meritocratic qualifications. Yet the meritocratic system itself is uneven, since apparently only certain qualities count. The deeper, more searching qualities are left almost totally out of consideration. For instance, Damfo, the master healer, in introducing the protagonist Densu to his art late on in the book, informs him that one of the penalties of being a healer is that you must live without respect:

> 'I'm not trying to discourage you,' Damfo said. 'But I must let you know the things a healer turns his back on are innumerable. These are things of the world. Not only things of the flesh, but also things touching the spirit. There's comfort. Wealth. There's also love, the respect of close ones. Even fame, the respect of distant people. Power among men. The satisfaction of being known wherever you go. These are the things that sweeten life for men. The healer turns his back on all of them.'
>
> 'Do you think I have not understood that?' Densu asked.
>
> 'It's hard to go away from the things everyone is going toward. It's lonely. It's hard to live the way a healer must necessarily live. It's hard to live without respect from others in the world.'
>
> 'Does a healer have no respect from others?' Densu asked.
>
> 'Not in the world as it is now.' (EAPH, pp. 110–11; Heinemann, pp. 90–1)

In order to adopt the healing vocation, Densu has to embrace what in many ways is a despised office. The fact that he is eventually willing to make this sacrifice marks him out as someone deeply at odds with the mainstream of Asante life. Indeed this is something we learn about him very early on, since the healer's philosophy supplies in him a long felt need, a lingering scepticism as to the binding force of aspirations the general population holds dear. Listen to him cogitating, in the opening pages of the novel, about the ultimate worth of the games in which he is obliged to participate:

It was this that had, in his fourteenth year, so disturbed the young man Densu. The question that had troubled him then had not left his mind in his twentieth year: what was the purpose of these games? Why did they seem so purposeless to him?

A whole community gathered every chosen year to take part in rituals of wholeness. But at the end of the ceremonies of wholeness a single individual was held up to be glorified by the whole community. Where was the root of wholeness in such a strange ritual of separation? Densu searched his feelings for some possible affirmation, for some hope that the things going on around him could make sense. But his feelings rebelled at being forced to look for sense in nonsense.

The truth Densu saw was a sharp image: a single winner riding over a multitude of losers. Unwilling to accept the meaning of the harsh image, Densu searched his mind for reasons to soften the truth he had seen. But his mind refused to show him any of the smooth roads to self-betrayal. The only reason he found in the nature of the games was something monstrous, a perversion that repelled him naturally, powerfully. (EAPH, p. 8; Heinemann, pp. 6–7)

Between the young man Densu and the cheering crowds at the games there is a deep gulf set. Densu is not, however, like the visionary heroes of some of Armah's earlier books, completely and irrevocably alone. There are others among both his elders and his contemporaries who share his sympathies. First and foremost among these, as we soon learn, are the eponymous healers themselves. But there are others who, though not healers themselves, share something of their hardy serenity, notably the nimble and resourceful Anan who, before he dies in his attempted escape from the trial scene, is able to lend Densu much moral support in his altercation with the society's more typical elements. Densu senses in Anan a deep, inventive confidence, and beyond that a core of abiding peace greater than any elation to be gained from a cheap victory over others. Anan's strengths are suggested in the early passage in which he takes Densu on a swimming expedition, and teaches him the art of under-water diving, using a hollowed-out bamboo cane as a sort of elementary snorkel. When they reach the river bed, Densu glances over to his friend, and

he had such a calm look on his face, a look so far beyond ordinary life, that Densu felt a sharp alarm. He moved closer and looked at his friend's throat. In the slow water with its fugitive lights and shadows running constantly into and from each other he could not tell if what he saw was breathing or not. (EAPH, p. 28; Heinemann, p. 23)

Later, when they are both recovering from their exertions on the bank:

> Densu took one more look at him lying there in the warm sand. The look on his face was serene, far beyond happiness. It was much the same look that had touched Densu's mind with panic at the bottom of the river, before he had understood it. (EAPH, pp. 28–9; Heinemann, p. 24)

Armah's typically precise description here enables us to learn something important about Anan, that during his brief life he has achieved what other, more eminent characters in the book will attain only at immense cost, peace with the inner depths of his own nature.

The deep divide in Asante society between those, like Anan, who prize peace and those, in the vast majority, who favour aggression, is not confined to the individual level. It is even reproduced at the pinnacle of Asante among the very Council of State. Any simplistic notions of the Asante as a proud, warlike people are countered by Armah's shrewd portrayal of a people sorely divided on the crucial issue as to whether or not to fight the British. In this Armah follows closely the recent findings of historians such as Ivor Wilks[2] who, relying on the eye-witness accounts of those such as the detained German missionaries, Ramseyer and Kühne,[3] who had an opportunity to observe the conflicts within the body politic, have given us a picture of a society within which the balance of opinion between competing war and peace factions was constantly changing. Throughout this period it would seem that the Asantehene, a moderate by temperament, was sore put to it to reconcile those who wished to pursue the war with increasing fervour and those like Asamoa Nkwanta, the Anantahene and even his own influential mother, who were sceptical of the value of resisting the British demands. Again, the popular impression of the tyrannical nature of traditional Asante is strongly countered in Armah's account. Armah relies here not on the more available instances of European apologetics, but rather on the detailed accounts of early visitors to Asante such as Bowdich and Dupuis, who give an impressive picture of a society replete in mechanisms to ensure that every shade of opinion is fully represented. Indeed the decision-making process, especially in external affairs, was both subtle and complex, and in the vital issue of the war the Asantehene himself carried only a very limited voice, for in Bowdich we read:

> The constitution requires or admits an interference of the Aristocracy in all foreign politics, extending even to a veto on the King's decision, but they watch rather than share the domestic administration, generally influencing it by their opinion, and never appearing to control it from authority; and their opinions on civil questions are

submitted with a deference, directly in contrast to their bold declarations on the subject of war and tribute, which amount to injunction.[4]

In Armah's account the main advocate of the peace party is Asamoa Nkwanta, a general of vast experience and prestige and by his title of 'ruler of the battles' hailed as the brightest star in the military firmament. Asamoa Nkwanta's disaffection from the war interest is well documented, and would appear to have originated in an incident several years previously when, on the death of Kwaku Dua I, the former Asantehene, in 1867, his nephew was accidentally killed in the traditional bloodbath intended to supply the deceased sovereign with slaves in the after-life. As a matter of historical fact, we know that the general's initial reaction to his bereavement had been a violent one, for, as Ivor Wilks informs us:

> Rejecting arguments that such actions on the death of the Asantehene were sanctioned by custom, Asamoa Nkwanta demanded retribution. When this was not forthcoming he mobilized his supporters and threatened to burn Kumasi.[5]

Eventually he was placated by the execution in vengeance of a number of the assassin's own family. Armah's version suppresses the less savoury aspects of the general's behaviour, and also brings the incident forward a few years so as to make it appear that it had occurred only very shortly before the British ultimatum. One repercussion of these earlier events had been to alienate the general from the environs of the Court, and in particular from the war party to which he had previously been allied. Again Armah exaggerates the significance of this development so as to make Asamoa Nkwanta the chief spokesman for the opposition to the Asante war interest. Structurally these modifications have great cogency, for they establish right in the sanctum of the state hierarchy an opposite pole to the official militarist ideals, and serve to articulate a degree of political scepticism which has its mystical equivalent in the spiritual activity of the healers.

There is one other reason why the character of Asamoa Nkwanta is so important. From the moment when we meet him, when he comes to the healer's village at Praso seeking advice, the great general acts as a living paradox: a military craftsman, a man of war who has increasingly become committed to the cause of peace. There is little doubt that the healers' influence serves to deepen his convictions in this respect, since abstention from violence is one of the foundations of their order. The anomalous position in which the general thus finds himself has the effect for us of raising the essential philosophical question of the validity of war as an instrument in the service of patriotic ideals. Throughout the novel Asante is portrayed as a nation at war, one which moreover is obliged to sustain a fighting posture in order to safeguard its territorial integrity. For instance, Amankwa Tia's expedition, which starts at the beginning of the novel as an enterprise of acquisition and conquest, has by the end transformed itself into a desperate rearguard action, a vital life-saving operation. To what extent can the healers, and Asamoa Nkwanka too with his newly acquired pacificism, condone the actions of an army which is defending itself against overwhelming odds? In the context of Armah's work this question has far-reaching implications, for it corresponds almost exactly to the query with which *Two Thousand Seasons* ended. There the seer Isanusi, regarded as a repository of spiritual wisdom with convictions not dissimilar to those of the healers, concluded with a slightly ambiguous pronouncement about the simplistic 'praise of arms'. In *The Healers* the same issue is raised perhaps more directly, in a manner which, however, refrains from eliciting an easy, complacent answer.

This clash of opinion and interest within Ashante society forms a framework within which the plot, a skilful compound of fiction and recorded fact, weaves its way, illuminating in its course various facets of the central philosophical debate and taking in a number of episodes identifiably drawn from the available historical sources. Densu, increasingly disgusted with the ugly competitive element in the games, deliberately contrives to forgo his advantages, hence coming second to the prince and heir-apparent Appia. His visible potential, however, is such that he is immediately approached by Ababio, a traitor and fifth columnist in the pay of the British at Cape Coast, with an offer of the kingship should he comply with the Europeans' plan to overrun Esuono. Densu protests, declaring that his loyalty rests with the healers and those who wish the dignity and independence of the State. After a visit to the healers' village, where he receives preliminary instruction in his chosen vocation from Damfo the master-healer, he is ambushed by Ababio's henchmen and, in a subsequent interview with his opponent, finds out that he is being blamed for the mysterious deaths of Appia and his mother Araba Jesiwa who have been struck down while wandering in the bush. Appia's body has been mutilated in such a way as to cast suspicion on Densu. However, during the ensuing trial by ordeal which has been rigged by Ababio and his collaborator Buntiu, Densu manages to escape back to the healers' village where he is welcomed by Damfo and his young daughter Ajoa, with whom Densu is gradually falling in love.

Thus ends the first phase of the story up to the appearance of Asamoa Nkwanta. A mere recitation of events, however, does scant justice to the effect of this opening section, which is to come to a definition of the art of the healers and of that which separates them from the majority of their countrymen. In opting for a life of relative seclusion among those dedicated to medical skill Densu is not merely responding to sentimentality, nostalgia, or immature idealism. The healers' way of life and outlook represent a feasible though demanding alternative to the practices of the tribe, one only embraced after a considerable period of training and a system of spiritual exercises almost as gruelling as Ignatius Loyola's. In his interviews with Damfo, Densu is introduced to the ground rules of the community. If he wishes to join he must refrain from alcoholic drink, violence and political involvement. These, however, are only the superficial mannerisms of commitment. At its heart lies an attitude to the quality of life which cuts at the root of Asante political organization. The novel's word for this is 'inspiration' by which is meant a creative alignment at odds with those who would force instinctual self-expression into alien channels, those whom the novel distinguishes as 'manipulators'.

Inspiration does not emerge merely as a vacuous mental quality, for in the practice of the healers it is grounded in a systematic therapeutic method. In the story this is illustrated by the case history of Araba Jesiwa, Appia's mother, who before her reported death has communicated to Densu something of her own indebtedness to the healers' guidance. Brought up among the royals of the Chief's household, she is educated into the idea that she is obliged to marry one of her own kind, and hence complies with a loveless match to an aristocrat with whom she is otherwise totally incompatible. The price she pays for her cowardice is sterility, or rather a series of disastrous miscarriages which leave her listless and despondent. After the last of these she approaches Damfo the healer for help. His advice to her is lucid and uncompromising: that the reason for her lack of maternal fulfilment has been her disloyalty to her own nature, and in particular to her former love for the darling of her youth, the humble carver Entsua. In order to achieve maternal satisfaction she has to do away with the encumbrances brought about by the mistaken demands of others ('the loved ones' of *The Beautyful Ones*), and attend instead to the promptings of her own heart.

Damfo's influence over Araba Jesiwa is portrayed as the very opposite of mere persuasion. As the princess later explains it to Densu, it is rather the systematic liberation of potentialities long dormant:

Glimpsing knowledge beyond experience, Densu asked her: 'Did he force you to change?'

The question touched a nerve in Jesiwa. It energized her.

'No. No force at all. That is a quality of Damfo's which makes him what he is. No deception, no force. He said to me: "Things go wrong when we do violence to ourselves. Yes, we have more than one self. The difficulty is to know which self to make the permanent one, and

which we should leave ephemeral. You set one of the passing selves
above your permanent self: that's doing violence to yourself. Things
will go wrong then, and you'll never know why as long as you remain in
the same situation and don't move out of it."

'In time I understood what I had to do. I had been false to myself. I
had to start being true to myself. It wasn't easy. In my blindness I had
almost killed my true self. I had embraced false selves and set them up
to dominate my real self. They were not even of my own making, these
false selves. They were pieces of other people, demands put out by
others to whom I used to give respect without stopping to think why.'
(EAPH, p. 84; Heinemann, p. 69)

The betrayal by Araba Jesiwa of her true interests in favour of a
borrowed ideal is but a picture in miniature of the situation in which the
whole of Asante society finds itself. The original ideal of Akan
'wholeness' has been ditched in a surfeit of social competitiveness and a
notion of purely individual advancement. The inevitable concomitants of
this process – slavery, the rise of an oligarchic ruling class, fragmentation
into jostling ethnic sub-groups – act as a blight on the whole texture of the
community's life. It is part of the healers' ultimate purpose to wean
society away from enslavement to these false idols, to which it is seemingly as addicted as were the emergent bourgeoisie of Armah's earlier
books to the bright gleam emanating from the cocktail cabinet and the
chrome panelling. That this analogy occurs is hardly surprising since
both sets of phenomena are seen as imports, a prestigious mimicry
of alient superfluities. But the healers, as Damfo later informs Densu,
have to move carefully, surrounded as they are by social ignominy,
and the resistance of those such as Ababio and Buntui, whose whole
activity is directed towards encouraging a whole society to be untrue
to itself.

The next phase of the story is also dominated by various applications of
the healers' art. Arriving in the healers' village, Densu to his amazement
discovers Araba Jesiwa, whom he like all of Esuano had thought dead,
being cared for by Damfo due to whose good offices she has been rescued
from slow extinction in the forest. Soon Damfo receives news of another
call on his attention. Asamoa Nkwanta, who has finally succumbed to the
doubts sown in his mind by his nephew's assassination, has come seeking
advice and awaits him in another healers' village called Praso, several days
journey up-river. After a long and perilous voyage in which even Araba
Jesiwa is transported by stretcher, Damfo encounters his new and eminent
patient in a clearing near the village. The therapy progresses slowly:
gradually, over several days, the healer works to win the general's
confidence, encouraging him to express his mind until they reach the
kernel of the matter, the ignoble death of the great man's nephew:

'That killing was the root of your illness then?'

'The root of everything,' he said hoarsely. 'They killed him like a slave.'

'Why?'

'What do you mean, why?'

'Do you know the reason for that death?'

'It's the custom.'

'Have you examined the custom that can result in so much murder?'

Asamoa Nkwanta's face gathered itself up into a puzzled mask of lines and shadows. His eyes narrowed, almost shut. Here was a man trying to master an idea still new to his ways of thought.

'Would you change the custom if you had the power?'

'No!' This was also vehement.

'Would your nephew have died if there hadn't been any such custom?'

'But I tell you the custom did not kill him.'

'I hear you. You say it was an accident, not a necessity of the custom.'

'Yes. It was an accident.'

'My question is, may not such accidents be prevented if . . .'

Asamoa Nkwanta finished for Damfo '. . . if the custom is abolished?' Those eyes of his looked so tired. 'What kind of world would it be then? A world without slaves?'

'Precisely,' said Damfo, calmly. 'A world without slaves.'

Asamoa Nkwanta had been ready to say something, but now he paused. He looked at Damfo's face. Then Asamoa Nkwanta laughed, even in his sorrow.

'A world without slaves! You might as well wish for a world without kings.'

'Yes, no slaves, no kings.' (EAPH, p. 213; Heinemann, p. 175)

The point is this: Asamoa Nkwanta, despite his celebrity, is in many ways taken to be a very typical figure, one who epitomizes the virtues and vices of a proud, imperialistic but morally complacent society. In him the process of self-questioning to which the Asante are currently prone is also enacted to an unusual degree. Damfo attempts to cure him by almost the same therapeutic technique as he had earlier used on the young Araba Jesiwa. By systematic discussion and gentle probing he slowly brings the patient round to a consideration of the reality of his own private nature. Like the princess the general has also been guilty of self-betrayal, but as his nature is so congruent with the public personality of the nation he serves, his betrayal also possesses a social dimension. It is not merely he, but also the whole of Asante, that has been untrue to itself. Thus Asamoa Nkwanta cannot begin to examine his own motivations without by the same token casting doubt on the very foundations of the empire, and especially the cherished institutions of kingship and slavery. It is at this juncture that the links between the healers' medical and their social

mission make themselves manifest. The kinds of disease to which Damfo
and his colleagues apply themselves are the products of that long process
of social disintegration which has brought Asante to the crisis in which it
currently finds itself.

The extent of that crisis soon becomes evident. Going down to the
river one morning Densu discovers a disorganized multitude of bewildered, frightened men crowding the bank in search of passage:
Amankwa Tia's routed army in retreat from their marauding expedition to the coast. In order to ensure a propitious crossing the harassed
commanders have recourse to the traditional method. A group of
terrified slaves, their tongues skewered in order to prevent execration
against the king, are brought to the river bank for instant execution.
With more ardour than sense Densu leaps to their rescue, thus provok-
ing the collective wrath of the army and his own almost certain death
were it not for the lucky arrival on the scene of Asamoa Nkwanta
himself, whom the commander immediately recognizes and whose plea
for Densu's release they respect.

The general's sojourn in Praso is not, however, to last much longer.
Meanwhile representatives have arrived from Kumasi to urge the commander's much needed return. He agrees on condition that Densu
accompany him in an intelligence capacity for which the young man's
command of English recommends him. Thus Densu begins that series of
scouting expeditions to various centres of British influence which are
used by the novelist as a means of giving us an insight into the state of
affairs in the colonial camp. The first of these is to Cape Coast itself,
Centre of British Administration in the Protectorate, where, dressed in
the healer's garb and bearing the enticement of a much-prized
aphrodisiac, Densu has the opportunity of viewing the famous durbar for
the chiefs of Fanteland convened by Sir Garnet Wolsey, the newly
arrived British commander, in what is now Victoria Park. The description of the durbar itself is unremarkable, following as it does Armah's
sources fairly closely. Afterwards, however, by gaining the ear of the
chief's linguist, Densu obtains entrance to the palace where a meeting of
the Fante Confederation, founded at Mankesim in 1871 for the purpose
of mutual defence, is taking place. A vivid impression is created of the
acute demoralization of these by now rather nominal chiefs, bereft of all
substantial authority by the British, caught between the Asante and
colonial power blocs, desperately attempting to play one off against the
other for the sake of a little peace of mind. The extent of their obligation
towards the governor at the castle gives them very little option but to
support Wolsey's expedition. The only available salve for their wounded
self-esteem is a pathetic bargaining for conditions, consisting of a cash

payment and a regular consignment of 'hot' drinks, several crates of which have just arrived at the palace and of which the chiefs proceed noisily to avail themselves, totally oblivious of Densu's intrusive presence.

If the Fantes are incapable of resisting British influence, east of the Volta the case is seen to be very different. Here the tribes are engaged in a running battle with their Awona neighbours on the opposite bank, in which they have craftily recruited the support of the Englishman, John Glover, with a promise that once the war is over they will combine under his leadership to join the expeditionary force at a point further up-river. Glover 'the father of the Hausas' was a freebooter, a popular and talented amateur, distrusted and despised by the ultra-professional Wolsey who was forced nevertheless to co-operate with him. As soon as Densu arrives at Ada he discerns the reasons for both Glover's influence and his impending disgrace, for indeed they are one and the same: the overweening, short-sighted conceit of the man. In order to suggest this quality, Armah has recourse to the novel's most dexterous and pointed deployment of source material. The novelist's source here can only have been the adulatory dispatch sent to the *New York Herald* by their correspondent, none other than the ubiquitous Henry Stanley, on his arrival on the Volta. Here is Stanley's wording, which Armah parodies;

> I soon discovered the sturdy form of Governor Glover striding hither and thither, and recognised his cool calm voice giving orders. He was superintending personally the loading of the Lady of the Lake for an up-river trip with ammunition; he was giving orders to a blacksmith; he was showing a carpenter what his day's duties might be; he was speaking to the engineer about his boiler; he was telling the colored captain how to be ready and what sand bar to avoid; he was assisting a man to lift a box of ammunition on his shoulders; he was listening to a Yoruba's complaint about some unfairness in the distribution of accoutrements; he was inspecting the crews of the steam launches; he was directing some of the steamboat men how to treat the wild bullocks; he was questioning the commissariat officer about his supplies; he was rebuking the Accra king, Taki, for the dilatoriness of his men; he was specifying the day's duties to a Hausa sergeant; he was here, there and everywhere; alert, active, prompt, industrious. He was general-in-chief, quartermaster, general, commissariat officer, military secretary, pilot, captain, engineer, general supervisor of all things, a most remarkable man, conductor of great and small things, a most remarkable man, and in short the impellent force of his army.[6]

Clearly very much Stanley's sort of man; was this one wonders how the freelance explorer extraordinary liked to view himself, a Jack of all trades who nevertheless mysteriously contrived to be master of all into the bargain? Armah is not nearly so impressed. Here, with its tone of mock homage, is Armah's version:

> Here he was, the white man who was known to have travelled through the lands beside the river even greater than the Firaw, the lands of the long, immense Kwarra to the east. Here he was, the man who had gone along the mysterious Kwarra and done what no mortal white man had ever hoped or dared to do even with help from thousands. Here he was, the man who knew himself a true magician when it came to getting black people to fight other black people for the profit of white people. Here he was, the one white man who could boast he could tell black men to do anything, no matter how difficult, and they would do it immediately out of love for him, Glover. Here he was, Glover the father of the Hausa fighters, protector of loving slaves. Here he was, Glover, he whose word was alone sufficient to inspire thirty thousand black men to rush delirious into the open jaws of death. Here he was, Glover the glorious, boastful one, Glover for-every-five-black-men-any-other-white-man-can-raise-I-alone-will-raise-hundreds. Here he was, the great white man. No need for the searcher to tire himself searching. Glover was visible as the sun this Saturday morning.
>
> Was it men still unloading crates from the river boats? Glover flitted like a wasp between the river's edge and the growing centre of his camp, making sure nothing would go wrong, that everything would be as perfect as the fantastic plans in his own head. Were men pitching new tents on the expanding outer reaches of the camp? Glover was there like a shot of lightning, giving them the most correct instructions about the proper tautness of each rope. Was it another line of men arriving from the river with bundles on their heads and shoulders? Glover was there, to show them which tent to put each bundle in. Glover was everywhere. Glover was the great white father, Glover was the omnipresent, omniscient god. (EAPH, pp. 311–12; Heinemann, pp. 255–6)

The fantastic prestige enjoyed by Glover is, however, an affair of a moment, as the anti-climactic sequel demonstrates. Bereft at the last moment of the support of the local tribesmen, who refuse to continue with the expedition up-river as long as their Awuna foes remain unquelled, he is forced to soldier on with a mere handful of faithful Hausas, arriving too late to play any decisive part in the campaign.

Faced with a steadily advancing army and seemingly insuperable odds, the Asante people collapse into superstition and morose, brooding fatalism. The various surviving legends which circulated around the environs of Kumasi during this period of tense anticipation are recorded and embellished by the novelist so as to produce almost a litany of petrified and confused speculation. Yet Armah's own account of these last few weeks serves in many ways to undermine the prevailing impression of helplessness, since the real cause of Asante vulnerability is shown to be their own dissension and self-distrust. Determined to resist the British incursion and yet anxious to save blood, Asamoa Nkwanta reiterates an already formulated defence plan which amounts to a devious form of passive resistance:

> All we need to do is keep to our plan. We shall let the white army from the south approach Kumase, but slowly. When the time comes to strike, the Juaben army under Nana Asafo Adjei will circle round the whites and cut off their escape route. We shall destroy their bridges, and oblige them to stay in these forests and fight till death. (EAPH, p. 341; Heinemann, p. 280)

He reckons without the urge to self-destruction that has seemingly overwhelmed the nation, together with the suspicion which he has personally aroused among those wary of his prominence. In her address to the War Council, the Queen Mother, well known for her passionate espousal of the peace interest, attempts to persuade her peers of the inevitability of the impending defeat, being none other than the just penalty visited upon them for previous greed:

> Ever since we began, we have depended not only on our strength, but on the help of the great one, Odomankoma Kwame, God of all creation. When our cause has been just he has given us victory. But what cause have we been fighting for these days? We have done so many things to bring the curse of God on our own heads, and God is punishing us. (EAPH, p. 339; Heinemann, p. 279)

In the presence of such crippling guilt, it is hardly surprising that the general's carefully prepared plan of defence fails to materialize. Poised on a ridge below Edwinase ready to strike as soon as the Juaben contingent to the south have closed the threatening net, Asamoa Nkwants discovers to his mortification that the will to fight has dissolved so far as to make even this amount of co-operation an impossibility:

> But from the south, the enemy's rear, all Asamoa Nkwanta heard this Saturday morning was the deep, gloomy silence of a universe grown indifferent to his hopes. He waited, hoping what he feared would prove to be untrue. But from behind the white lines no sound came to reassure his still grieving soul, and he saw no sign. (EAPH, p. 345; Heinemann, p. 284)

It is only on his return to Kumasi that the general discovers that in his absence the Queen Mother has persuaded the Asantehene to yield to the British rather than countenance the political repercussions of Asamoa Nkwanta's success.

What is the authorial attitude to the Asante capitulation? The question is clearly relevant in the light of the sustained critique of violence and aggression which pervades the book. If violence, as the healers clearly believe, is a symptom of a deep social disease, are passivity and surrender to be taken as signs of health? The problem is a convoluted one, since there are moments in the text which would seem to lend support to either view. For instance, some time before the final holocaust, the return of Amankwa Tia's dejected army to Kumasi after their coastal exploits is described in terms which suggest eloquently the terrible pathos of defeat:

> But what a sad homecoming this one was for the army! What a terrible accounting faced the nation! A procession of warriors passed through Kumase, Kumase the virgin capital, Kumase the impregnable stronghold, Kumase the evergreen garden. But this was no proud procession of victory. Those who came out of their houses to welcome their returning warrriors saw only a slow, sorrowful march of survivors whose every step cried a single message: to death alone belonged the victory in this war.
>
> Tongue-tied were the singers of victorious songs of praise. What could they sing of? And for whom to hear? Those who had looked forward to the cruel pleasure of taunting long lines of captives brought back from the battlefields grew sad. Here were no captives to be taunted and insulted. Here were only bereaved survivors. Nephews in all the strength of their youth had gone to this war with forty companions. Now they returned alone carrying forlorn bundles to remind those alive of beloved ones whom death had swallowed away from home. (EAPH, p. 297; Heinemann, p. 243)

The paradox of values is very deep here. The army's retreat is clearly seen as an instance of lack of nerve, yet there are hints – for instance, that phrase about 'long lines of captives brought back from the battlefields' – which would appear to be distinctly disparaging of the consequences which would have accrued from a possible victory. Moreover, retrenchment is in direct compliance with Asamoa Nkwanta's already formulated policy of passive resistance and would even seem to be pertinent to his design of drawing the British armies into the trap of invading Ashanti territory.

The contradiction in tone is acute, yet capable of a kind of resolution. It is Damfo the healer who, on withdrawing from the war front on completion of his work, sets the context inside which the dilemmas facing Ashanti territory must be solved. Indeed the paradox we have already noted in the authorial attitude is also observable to a certain extent in the healer's own behaviour. In returning one of the army's prize leaders to fighting shape and then releasing him to unleash violence, however reluctantly, on the advancing British line, is he not renouncing his sacred trust as a man of peace? When this discrepancy is put to him, Damfo feels obliged to counsel realism. After all Asamoa Nkwanta is by trade a general, a servant of the State who, as such, is called upon to fulfil certain requirements. To ask him to refrain from acting in his country's defence would be to demand that he should violate an important aspect both of his calling and of the social network which sustains it. Like everybody else the healers are forced to achieve whatever they can within the conditions which currently obtain, hoping in the long run to work towards the ultimate ideals of brotherhood and peace:

> Healing is work, not gambling. It is the work of inspiration, not manipulation. If we the healers are to do the work of helping bring our whole people together again, we need to know such work is the work of a community. It cannot be done by an individual. It should not depend on any single person, however heroic he may be. And it can't depend on people who do not understand the healing vocation – no matter how good such people may be as individuals.
>
> The work of healing is work for inspirers working long and steadily in a group that grows over the generations, until there are inspirers, healers wherever our people are scattered, able to bring us together again. (EAPH, p. 328; Heinemann, p. 270)

The distant perspective – complete social cohesion, peace both within the community and the individual mind – is deftly suggested by the culmination of the plot. In sorrow of heart, Densu retires from Kumasi, but not before he has witnessed the execution of the bully Buntui in a manner befitting his crimes. Passing through Praso he observes the burning of the healers' village by disgruntled elements within its midst. Eventually, after rejoining Damfo and Ajoa, he makes his way to the palace at Esuano, only to find that his arch-enemy Ababio has now been enstooled as chief. No sooner has Densu confronted him than Ababio has the young man arrested for the alleged murder of Appia. Hauled off to Cape Coast for a trial in the British manner, he is rescued at the eleventh hour by Araba Jesiwa who, now well both in body and soul, is able to testify to Buntui's guilt and Ababio's complicity. After the latter's arrest, the British expeditionary force embarks from the Protectorate, sent off by a carnival of rejoicing from the varied ethnic groups gathered in this place for a campaign intended originally as divisive, but giving rise in the event to a paradoxical cohesion:

> Here were Opobo warriors from the east, keeping at a distance from their neighbours from Bonni. Here were Hausas brought by Glover from the Kwarra lands. Here were mixed crowds with men from Dahomey, Anecho, Atakpame, Ada, Ga and Ekuapem. There were a few Efutu men, and numbers of Fantse policemen in ill-fitting new uniforms. Here were tough, hardened Kru men from the west, Mande and Temne men from even farther west, and the fierce Sussu men inseparable from their swords of war.

All heard the music of these West Indians who had turned the white men's instruments of the music of death to playing such joyous music. All knew ways to dance to it, and a grotesque, variegated crowd they made, snaking its way through the town, followed by a long, crazy tail of the merely idle, the curious, and the very young. (EAPH, p. 376; Heinemann, p. 309)

In their determination to set the black race against itself and hence exacerbate the already severe process of fragmentation, the British have only succeeded in bringing it, however fleetingly, together. A mercurial conclusion, perhaps, but one which serves to project poetically the longed for ideal of wholeness, from which the rest of the novel marks a retreat. Thus, figuratively, the end of history rejoins its beginning, and, in terms of a circular vision of time here latent, though simultaneously localized, the cycle at length becomes complete.

REFERENCES AND NOTES

1. Ayi Kwei Armah, *The Healers* (Nairobi: East African Publishing House, 1978; London: Heinemann Educational Books, 1979). Page references in the text are given for both editions.
2. Ivor Wilks, *The Asante in the Nineteenth Century* (Cambridge: Cambridge University Press, 1975).
3. F. A. Ramseyer and J. Kühne, *Four Years in Ashante* (London, 1875).
4. T. E. Bowdich, *Mission from Cape Coast to Ashanti* (London, 1819; n.e., London: F. Cass, 1966).
5. Wilks, *op. cit.*, p. 497.
6. Alan Lloyd, *The Drums of Kumasi* (Harlow: Longman, 1964), p. 122.

Conclusion

▼▼▼▼▼▼▼▼▼▼▼▼▼▼▼▼▼▼▼▼▼▼▼▼▼▼▼▼▼▼▼▼

THE novelist, James Joyce claimed, has a duty to be impartial.[1] An unimpeachable statement many would say, and one from which many subsequent critics of the fictional medium have taken their cue. It is, however, the sort of assertion which is only meaningful within the social and historical context against which Joyce himself was writing, the context of a cosmopolitan society, economically diversified with a wide cultural base drawing on a tradition of letters and literary discourse centuries old, and wedded to the idea, either undiluted or at one remove, that art exists for its own sake in a zone free from the pressures of commercial or political life. The piety of this orthodox view of the role of fiction is often repeated; subconsciously it is taken under the skin by generations of readers, students and scholars, many of whom hardly spare a thought for the evident corollary of this species of argument, which must be that, in other societies under a different set of cultural circumstances, another view of the matter must presumably be allowed to prevail.

Despite this, the sanctities and susceptibilities implicit in Joyce's view are carried over all too often into a field of study quite removed from the conditions which gave rise to his statement. To take one notable instance, critics of the work of Chinua Achebe have always been at pains to demonstrate his complete historical objectivity, the scrupulous distance that his work maintains from mere polemic.[2] True enough, Achebe is a singularly fair-minded artist, one whose peculiar strength lies in his refusal to over-simplify social issues for the sake of a cheap, easily attained victory. Yet Achebe is an African artist who has decided views on the obligations under which he works and a sense of social mission; his own conception of the function and emphasis of his work does not altogether coincide with the ideas which his critics have on the matter. The same may be said of a number of his anglophone contemporaries. Wole Soyinka's casual aside to the Stockholm Conference that 'a tiger does not proclaim his tigritude; he pounces'[3] has often been mistaken as a disclaimer of social responsibility. Yet his subsequent statements on the matter have given no weight to the view that his confirmed rejection of Négritude as a doctrine implies any form of purism over the issue of the relation of literature to political and social reality.[4]

Ayi Kwei Armah is a decade younger than either Achebe or Soyinka, an artist of a younger and perhaps more ardent generation, a man who, as the first chapter of this study was intended to show, has been subjected to influences which were likely to carry him even further away from the reassuring aesthetic pastures of the conventional novel towards the more austere regions of functionalist art. His work can be seen not merely as a response to the cultural evolution of the African continent, but more crucially as an attempted answer to a question whose urgency becomes even more pressing: what, after all, is the purpose of the novel, above all of that couched in the English language, in the setting of a post-colonial African nation state? The very question is sufficient to raise a few quizzical and scholarly eyebrows. The rejoinder may well be put: what purpose, functionally conceived, can any art worthy of the name be deemed to serve under any circumstances, beyond those of entertainment and the satisfaction of certain specifically aesthetic instincts?

Yet in countries in which the English language is the mother tongue of only a very few, where the rate of literacy in any language is far from complete, where, under the pressures of social transformation, every issue, however private and sacrosanct, is likely sooner or later to assume a political form, the question of the novel's purpose – its actual, everyday justification – cannot long be avoided. Even those writers who have seemingly tried hardest to fight free from the claims of invective or mere instruction, have been forced at some point to formulate some kind of conception of the social role which they as artists understand themselves to be playing. A seminal, indeed a classic, statement on this question may be found in Chinua Achebe's 'The novelist as teacher', originally an address delivered to the conference on Commonwealth Literature held in Leeds in 1964. Talking about the traumatic effect on the Nigerian psyche of the feelings of inferiority inflicted during the colonial period, he goes on to say:

Here, then, is an adequate revolution for me to espouse – to help my society regain its belief in itself and put away the complexes of the years of denigration and self-denigration. And it is essentially a question of education in the best sense of that word. Here, I think, my aims and the deepest aspirations of my society meet. For no thinking African can escape the pain of the wound in our soul. You have all heard of the African personality; of African democracy, of the African way to socialism, of negritude, and so on. They are all props we have fashioned at different times to help us get on our feet again. Once we are up we shall not need any of them any more. But for the moment it is in the nature of things that we may need to counter racism with what Jean-Paul Sartre has called an anti-racist racism, to announce not just that we are as good as the next man but that we are better.[5]

This statement is remarkable, not merely for its candour and sensitivity, but also for its essential realism. The African writer works against a background of often awesome social and material deprivation: hunger, displacement, human stress. These are all needs which demand instant and sustained attention, but not such as the professional writer is in any real position to alleviate. The committed writer thus has perforce to view his duty in different terms. Poverty he is unlikely in any sense to relieve, but there is an ingrained poverty of the spirit and the cultural will, a chronic failure of the communal imagination, for the tending of which his craft and skills are peculiarly relevant. He comes from a society wracked not merely by physical distress and inequality, but by a debilitating self-distrust which cuts at the very roots of a people's self-assertion. The process, as Achebe suggests, begins perhaps in the schoolroom with its until recently slavish indoctrination of foreign influences, but goes in fact much farther back to the first disastrous sense of shame felt by the peoples of West Africa at the eruption of manifestations of a superficially more powerful culture. The hurt runs deep, the running sores only suggesting at the gross infection of the whole social organism. It is here that the writer can help, applying his healing art and bracing the spirit by reference to a vision of social confidence sufficient to dispel the gloom of accumulated self-loathing.

Emphatic as Achebe's ideas are in this direction, it is difficult if not impossible to discern the connections between his theory and his practice. True, the first section of his extraordinary novel, *Things Fall Apart*,[6] provides us with an excellent and compelling picture of one West African civilization in all its excellent repleteness before the disintegration of the colonial period wrought its undoing. The subsequent sections, however, serve to demonstrate not so much how external pressures broke that coherence up as how certain implicit and salient weaknesses in the social set-up led the culture progressively to work its own undoing. The lesson, in so far as there is one, which the novel provides is a self-corrective rather than a self-assertive one, the fatal flaws present beneath the originally perfect surface becoming increasingly obvious under the pressures of social stress. Moreover, just as Achebe's vision of the African past is a severely critical one, so does he refrain from supplying any positive or suggestive foreshadowing of the future, his fourth and contemporary novel, *A Man of the People*,[7] being as censorious of the vain aspirations of the young ingenuous idealist, Odili, as it is of the thorough-going corruption of his elder rival, Chief Nanga. Achebe, it is true, wishes to teach, but his lessons are harsh and unbending, his rod sternly corrective of any tendency towards self-celebration. Achebe, perhaps, belongs to the puritan, the Protestant tradition of the novel in

English (despite his avowed catholicism): his notion of social salvation being attuned to the progressive improvement and self-scrutiny of the individual mind. He has no compelling social vision to offer us: the way on is as impenetrable as the mazes of his protagonist Chief Ezeulu's mind.[8]

Armah too has offered us vistas which lead back to the distant past, but his work began with a fearless look at the present, and opens finally on the prospect of a future. His first three novels examine with great astuteness both the malaise affecting a confused and image-tossed post-colonial society, and the seemingly irresolvable impasse in which its more conscientious intellectuals find themselves. It was this shrewdness that was mistaken for bitterness by his early reviewers, this honesty that was taken for rancour. Armah has, however, chosen not to remain with his first essential preparatory task of depicting the morass into which his people (and other peoples who have suffered similar historical experiences) still find themselves, but has now turned to attempt to indicate the way out. Since the genesis of the problem coincided with a departure from inherited, ancestral norms, the enterprise clearly involved at some stage an imaginative return to the period at which the desertion took place, not in a mood of nostalgia, or even primarily one of recrimination, but simply in order to sort out the strengths from the weaknesses of the society, the exact point of junction between authenticity and self-betrayal. The result has been a heightened form of the historical novel. Yet it would also be true to say that Armah is not a writer who strikes one as possessing a fascination with the past for its own sake. The object here is purely and simply to enable the envisaged audience to get its bearings, to achieve a sense of direction preparatory to the supreme task of reconstruction. And reconstruction here must be seen not simply as a poetic fancy, a roseate glow suffusing the closing pages of his more recent books, and intended, perhaps, to counteract the depressing culmination of his earlier two novels. More than that, it is part and parcel of the novel's renewed purpose, a structure and a vigour that it gains from what Soyinka calls 'the visionary reconstruction of the past for the sake of social direction'.[9]

As already stated in the preface, Armah is a profoundly, one might also say instinctively, democratic artist. By this I do not mean that he is wedded to a commitment to any political system or hard-and-fast set of beliefs, but that he has a deep and sophisticated sense of the audience for which he writes, and of his obligations towards them. That audience – there is no point in beating about the bush on this point – is identifiably and almost exclusively African. To the extent that European readers and critics have taken cognisance of his work, this must be seen as a spin-off

or by-product of the central process embodied in the books, the trans-
mission of cultural confidence by a writer speaking directly to his people
by means of the fictional medium. In these circumstances the critic of
whatever nationality must tread warily. There are a number of factors
here which embarrass and complicate the task of assessment. To begin
with, if Armah's books have a social purpose, then they must be judged
with reference to it. If they are to be seen not simply as works of art but
also as active, efficient social instruments, then efficacy, rather than
abstract excellence becomes a valid criterion. If the novels are intended in
some measure to persuade, then how persuasive are they? To work at all
they must convince, but not only as an achieved masterpiece is normally
said to convince, by its rightness, its proportion, but, to some extent at
any rate, just as an argument convinces, by its sheer persuasive force. To
apply these criteria at all is admittedly to fly in the face of established
critical norms, to outrage many of the most cherished canons of Western
taste, but, as we have already argued, Western taste is not here in
question, nor is the critical consensus usually invoked in these matters in
reviews and faculties necessarily the most appropriate one.

Thus finally one comes to the unavoidable question with which we
began, how good a novelist is Ayi Kwei Armah? Disregarding for the
moment the dictates and fluctuation of critical fashion, what are his
enduring merits and the reservations that have ultimately to be recorded
against him? The strengths of his early books are, I should hope, obvious; a great narrative vividness, a quick and flexible technical resource, a
disturbing yet always controlled evocation of individual human distress,
whether shared in a relationship or, more usually, endured in solitude.
One recalls particularly the daily dread of the man in *The Beautyful Ones*
as he approaches the appalling yet ineluctable problem of attempting to
reconcile his moral scruples with the needs and claims of his family;
Baako's horrifying descent into madness in *Fragments*, and, in *Why Are
We So Blest?*, Solo's desperate attempts to fashion a meaningful relationship with a younger fellow African so like himself in temperament but yet
so wary of his independence. These are bright individual touches which
affect the sensitive reader with moments of recognition and startling
empathy – they remain in the memory as extraordinary life-like recrea-
tions of human pain. But they are the kind of creative elements which the
conventional critical tradition can easily accommodate. When we come
to the last two books, we are faced with an acute problem of critical
readjustment. The plural voice and emphasis clearly precludes precisely
the sort of concentrated, singular power we appreciated before: even in
The Healers, despite the prominence of Densu, there is no protagonist
with which we can immediately identify as we could with Baako. The

historical distance also to a certain extent intensifies the problem: neither Densu nor Damfo are creatures of our world, their problems being of quite another order, despite the implied analogies with the modern world we have already noted. More than this: in both these latter books, there are characters with whom we are especially required not to identify: the whites, for instance, in *Two Thousand Seasons*, or Buntui in *The Healers*. There are further disadvantages. With the difference in time, something of the earlier vividness also indubitably disappears and, with it, some of the effect of the style. There are moments in both these books which drag their feet, where we have a marked feeling of the writer labouring to maintain an interest over much that is repetitious or even dull. To some extent this is a subjective matter, but reference to the text will easily establish points at which two adjacent adjectives simply reiterate one another without adding to the sense, or where a high-sounding phrase is brought in to cover up an illogicality of thought, or even, in the less charitable passages, a certain meanness of emotion.

Has Armah then paid too high a qualitative price for the dogmatic thrust he introduces into the more recent novels? To some extent, yes. But we are here in great danger of letting our quibbles about the minutiae of the text interfere with the powerful sense that we must have of the cumulative dramatic power of both these books, their drive and momentum, together with the remarkable refurbishing of the novelist's craft that they represent. Totally to alter the standard way of interpreting the events of nineteenth-century Ashanti, and to connect this with an active compelling historical world-view, is no mean feat. Nor is the encapsulation of a thousand years of racial history in a novel form which imitates the traditional oracular forms of the chronicler's art. As a whole both these books are indubitably powerful and persuasive: the cogency of the case they make is undeniable. As instruments of persuasion, popular yet with a certain gravity of utterance, they are certainly effective – almost, one might argue, too effective in the way in which they shape opinion and potentially direct social action. This is the climax and the culmination of Armah's work to date, embracing a purpose beyond the despondency of *The Beautyful Ones* or the agonized self-scrutiny of the earlier books: it is a bold attempt at the creation both of a new novelistic form and of a fresh sensibility, one valid not merely for the individual reader in his study or schoolroom, but for the community at odds with itself, and sorely in need of light. To succour this need, the novels of Ayi Kwei Armah have so far supplied a resolute and probing beam.

REFERENCES AND NOTES

1. For a defence of this position see James Joyce, *Stephen Hero* (London: Jonathan Cape, 1944).

2. See for instance Gerald Moore, *Seven African Writers* (London: Oxford University Press, 1962).

3. From 'The Writer in a Modern African State', in Per Wästberg (ed.), *The Writer in Modern Africa* (Uppsala, 1968).

4. See especially Soyinka, *Literature, Myth and the African World*, op. cit.

5. Chinua Achebe, 'The Novelist as Teacher', in John Press (ed.), *Commonwealth Literature* (London: Heinemann Educational Books, 1965), p. 204.

6. Chinua Achebe, *Things Fall Apart* (London: Heinemann Educational Books, 1958).

7. Chinua Achebe, *A Man of the People* (London: Heinemann Educational Books, 1966).

8. In Chinua Achebe, *Arrow of God* (London: Heinemann Educational Books, 1964).

9. Soyinka, op. cit., p. 114.

Bibliography

▼▼▼▼▼▼▼▼▼▼▼▼▼▼▼▼▼▼▼▼▼▼▼▼▼▼▼▼▼▼▼▼

The Works of Ayi Kwei Armah

For convenience, British, American, and African editions, where obtainable, have been listed; page references given in the text are to the standard British edition, and sometimes also to that of the East African Publishing House.

NOVELS

The Beautyful Ones Are Not Yet Born (Boston: Houghton Mifflin, 1968; London: Heinemann Educational Books, 1969). Translated into Swahili as *Wema Hawajazaliwa* (Nairobi: Heinemann (East Africa), 1976).

Fragments (Boston: Houghton Mifflin, 1970; London: Heinemann Educational Books, 1974; Nairobi: East African Publishing House, 1974).

Why Are We So Blest? (New York: Doubleday, 1972; London: Heinemann Educational Books, 1974; Nairobi: East African Publishing House, 1974).

Two Thousand Seasons (Nairobi: East African Publishing House, 1973; London: Heinemann Educational Books, 1979).

The Healers (Nairobi: East African Publishing House, 1978; London: Heinemann Educational Books, 1979).

This study has chosen to concentrate on Armah as a novelist, but he is also a short story writer, polemicist, and poet, and the following selective list may help readers who are interested to locate texts.

SHORT STORIES

'Yaw Manu's Charm', *Atlantic* (May 1968).
'The Offal Kind', *Harper's Magazine* (January 1969).

POEM

'Aftermath', in Kofi Awoonor and G. Adali Mortty (eds), *Messages: Poems from Ghana* (London: Heinemann Educational Books, 1970).

POLITICAL THEORY

'African socialism: utopian or scientific', in *Présence Africaine*, no. 64 (Paris, 1967), pp. 6–30.

Secondary Sources

A selective list of critical articles and reviews from British, American and African periodicals.

Folarin, Margaret, 'An additional comment on Ayi Kwei Armah's *The Beautyful Ones Are Not Yet Born*', in E. D. Jones (ed.), *African Literature Today*, Vol. 5 (London: Heinemann Educational Books, 1971), pp. 116–29.

Fraser, Robert, 'The American background in *Why Are We So Blest?*', in E. D. Jones (ed.), *African Literature Today*, Vol. 9 (London: Heinemann Educational Books, 1978).

Hayman, Ronald, *The Novel Today, 1967–75* (Harlow: Longman, 1976), p. 49.

Jones, Eldred, review of *The Beautyful Ones* in *African Literature Today*, Vol. 3 (London: Heinemann Educational Books, 1969), pp. 55–7.

Kariara, Jonathan, in *Zuka* (Nairobi), no. 4 (December 1969), pp. 57–8.

K. W., 'The uses of nausea', *West Africa*, no. 2691 (London, 28 December 1968), pp. 1540–1.

Mahood, Molly, 'West African writers in the world of Frantz Fanon', *English Department Workpapers* (Ghana, Cape Coast), Vol. 1 (March 1971).

Moore, Gerald, 'Armah's second novel', *Journal of Commonwealth Literature*, Vol. ix, no. 1 (August 1974), p. 71.

Nicholson, Mary, 'The organization of symbols in Ayi Kwei Armah's *The Beautyful Ones Are Not Yet Born*', *Asemka*, Vol. 1, no. 2 (Ghana, December 1974), pp. 7–16.

Noble, R. W., review in *Journal of Commonwealth Literature*, no. 9 (July 1970), pp. 117–19.

Obiechina, Emmanuel, review in *Okike* (Nigeria, Nsukka) (April 1971), p. 52.

Ogunbesan, Kolawale, 'Symbol and meaning in *The Beautyful Ones Are*

Not Yet Born', in E. D. Jones (ed.), *African Literature Today*, Vol. 7 (London: Heinemann Educational Books, 1975).

Soyinka, Wole, *Myth, Literature and the African World* (Cambridge: Cambridge University Press, 1976), pp. 107–16.

Yankson, Kofi, '*The Beautyful Ones Are Not Yet Born*. An anatomy of shit', *English Department Workpapers* (Ghana, Cape Coast) Vol. 1 (1971).

Index

▼▼▼▼▼▼▼▼▼▼▼▼▼▼▼▼▼▼▼▼▼▼▼▼▼▼▼▼▼▼▼